OPEN HANDS
OPEN HEART

COMMENDATIONS

This book is superb. First because it is about our loving, generous

I am pleased to commend Ifor William's book for two good reasons. One, because my wife and I have observed Ifor and Penny for 17 years and know them to be people of faith and integrity. Two, because what has been written is such an encouragement from life as well as scripture to allow Jesus to be the Lord of our finances. This is biblical doctrine 'fleshed out' in the nitty gritty of real life experience.

We are challenged to be obedient servants, stewards not owners, and to put our trust in His promises; He who outrageously abandoned Himself in love, filling us with the Spirit of adoption and shaping us into His likeness, that we in turn might abandon ourselves in outrageous and generous giving. With joy! Read on and prepare for heart-searching....

Roy Godwin. Executive Director, The Ffald y Brenin Trust

This book is a 'must read'; the personal story of Ifor Williams, who led a Baptist church which became increasingly generous through a journey of faithful obedience over 20 years. Brimming with Bible passages interspersed with amazing anecdotes, the book reads like a modern day Acts of the Apostles. The book's message, if received with faith and applied, will prove to be a thrilling life changer. What God did for Ifor, his family and the church he led, can be done in us. 'God has no favourites.'

Ben Davies. Senior Pastor of Bracknell Baptist/ Bracknell Family/ Kerith Community Church 1964-2007

"*Open hands Open Heart*" has arisen from two basic convictions: the Scriptures reveal the heart of God; and we discover His goodness and faithfulness when we step out in faith to do His will. Ifor makes this abundantly clear in the most personal way and his challenge deserves to be widely embraced.

Rob James. Baptist Pastor,
Church and Media Consultant EA Wales.

Ifor's book blends together his own life lessons and biblical principles applied over time. With lots of practical advice rooted in Scripture, Ifor is able to gently engage the reader with the subject of living generously without being preachy. His own personal stories balanced with Bible teaching ensure that there is something for new and older Christians alike which are graciously offered to the reader who wants to live with an open hand and open heart. I commend this book to you and pray that it will be a gift to both reader and local church.

Revd Simeon Baker. Director of Mission,
Baptist Union of Wales

OPEN HANDS
OPEN HEART

Discovering God's
Amazing Generosity

Ifor Williams

 GENEROUS HEART

DEDICATION

*To the members and friends, over the years,
of Broad Haven Baptist Church.
You joined me on the journey.
You will always have a special place in my heart.*

CONTENTS

ACKNOWLEDGEMENTS

I owe a great debt of thanks to many people who have helped with this book. First and foremost, Mike Plaut, who encouraged me to write what I was teaching, and whose gentle, patient and challenging persistence made sure it happened; to Bruce Collins, who read the first draft many years ago and encouraged me to keep going; to Kerry Steed, who advised me to 'write as you preach'; to the Baptist Union of Wales, who graciously allowed me a Sabbatical in order to complete the writing; to Becky Matyus and Emma Wright my daughter and niece, who gave invaluable advice whilst also editing and proof reading; to Phil Bishop and Gina Stabile-Jones, my friends at 'Generous Heart' who made the whole process of publishing so much easier; to Keith Tondeur who encouraged me more than he will ever know, and who kindly agreed to write the foreword; to the many other friends and colleagues who were good enough to read and comment on the final draft, some of whose commendations have been printed.

To our amazing children Kevin, Mary, Becky, Katie and Lucy, who know what it's like to be pastor's kids, and who kept me sane over the years – thank you for sharing with me in 'giving and receiving'; and finally but most importantly to Penny, my wife and best friend who has been with me through it all, sharing the tears and the joys, and who still loves me!

FOREWORD
BY KEITH TONDEUR OBE

When Ifor wrote and asked me to look at his book I did not expect to be completely blown away - nor to read it through in one go! I have never met Ifor but soon felt I was really getting to know him as I read through his book. I have seen many books on giving over the years, ranging from glib "prosperity" type teaching to dry almost threatening tomes. But Ifor's love of Jesus flows from this eminently readable book and it is this which gives it such power. The combination of biblical teaching and personal example is excellent and I can certainly say that this is one of the best and most readable books on giving that I have ever read.

I think this book stands out from others for two main reasons. Firstly because throughout the book there is excellent biblical teaching that Ifor has expertly slotted in to the chapters in just the right places. Secondly, Ifor has skilfully managed to combine this teaching with practical and moving examples, both from his personal and church life, to demonstrate the many positive impacts of giving generously.

Throughout the book he takes us on a journey which will encourage all who read it to take steps to change their priorities and thus become more like Jesus in doing so. Whether it is in changing our attitudes to become more spiritually focused in our day-to-day lives, or helping us understand more clearly about the grace of giving, Ifor manages to convince us that this is something that we want to do.

As I know from personal experience, writing and talking about money and giving is an incredibly difficult thing to get right as there is a tendency for all of us to be defensive and feel somewhat guilty about such issues. But this book climbs above these matters and by using personal examples - including his struggles to overcome worldly desires - Ifor encourages us to take the next steps on our eternal journey.

Ifor clearly demonstrates that as we give generously we leave a space that God can fill to over-flowing with love, forgiveness and compassion. This is such an example in our materialistic world.

We demonstrate our faith by action and Ifor shows that if we follow biblical teaching and have a genuine love for Jesus, it will result in generous actions that will bring positive benefits to many - not least the givers themselves. It will of course also have positive eternal blessings.

This is a wonderful, powerful and moving book which needs to be widely read. Church leaders should also read it, as I think it will encourage many to get copies for their congregations, as this is often a difficult subject for leaders to teach.

I cannot speak too highly of this book and commend it to you.

Keith Tondeur OBE
Formerly President of Credit Action - the Christian money education charity.

INTRODUCTION

This book is about letting go and learning to give generously from the heart. Letting go of whatever or whoever is more important in your life than Jesus. Learning to give to God, to others, to the poor, as God prompts. Learning to supply the needs of others, and trusting God to look after your needs. Learning to make sacrifices so that others may be blessed. Learning to put Jesus first, others second, yourself third. Learning to follow Jesus on his terms rather than our own. Learning that everything we have belongs to God, and therefore holding lightly to all we possess, being ready to let go whenever the Master prompts us. It's about joy and generosity. The joy of giving. Discovering what Paul meant when he wrote that *"God loves a cheerful giver."* (2 Cor 9:7).

Generous giving begins with God. Imagine holding out your hands, palm uppermost. The left hand represents the hand of God, who always gives generously with an open hand. The Father let go of that which was more precious to him than anything else, and gave up his Son to be crucified. *"God so loved the world that he gave…"* (Jn 3:16). Giving is what God does. It's his nature. And whenever God gives, he gives generously, abundantly, extravagantly. The God of love is himself the originator of generous love.

Now look at your right hand which represents mankind. Man was made in the image of God, with the ability to give, as God gives. But in Genesis 3 we read that Eve reached out and took what did not belong to her, and then gave some of the forbidden fruit to Adam. In doing so her ability to give became corrupted, as she gave her husband a poisoned gift which would bring about his ruin. Close your right hand into a fist. This is what sin has done to mankind. Instead of giving we take. Instead of sharing we keep. This is now second nature to us. Not the nature or image of God in which we were created, but the fallen nature of mankind.

The Bible tells us that Christ died and rose again to redeem our selfish nature. This book explores through the Bible and my own experience, and that of my family and the church at Broad Haven in Pembrokeshire, where I ministered for over 20 years, how God takes our clenched fist and gently opens our fingers one by one, helping us to let go, and then teaching us to give with an open hand and an open heart, redeeming the image of God in which we were made. This has always been God's plan for mankind.

"If there is a poor man among your brothers in any of the towns of the land that the Lord your God is giving you, do not be hardhearted or tightfisted toward your poor brother. Rather be openhanded and freely lend him whatever he needs… give generously to him and do so without a grudging heart; then because of this the Lord your God will bless you in all your work and in everything you put your hand to. There will always be poor people in the land. Therefore I command you to be openhanded toward your brothers and toward the poor and needy in your land." (Dt 15:7-11).

PART 1

GIVING AND TAKING

1 The God Who Gives

The Bible says that '*God loves a cheerful giver*' (2 Cor 9:7), but for many years my personal experience of giving was anything but cheerful. The idea of 'giving' to God, the church or those in need was a completely new concept for me when I became a Christian in my late teens. I had no church background, and for many years I struggled with the whole question of giving. Quite simply, when the offering plate came round during a church service, I had absolutely no idea what I should put in it. Other people seemed to put in a handful of change, and I would do the same, but whatever I gave, it never felt right. Sometimes I would feel guilty about not giving enough. Then I would go to the other extreme and give more generously, not from the heart, but simply out of guilt. Whatever I gave, I always had the sense that it was not enough.

One day in 1986 it all came to a head. My wife Penny and I were attending Spring Harvest, the Christian family conference held at Butlins holiday camp in Minehead. Literally thousands of people were streaming into a huge marquee, looking forward to the worship and inspired teaching, but Penny and I were round the back of the marquee, embroiled in a huge row.

It was the final night of the conference, and as usual there was going to be an appeal that evening for some worthy cause. At the time I was studying for the ministry, and we had precious little money, but a dog, a cat, and three children to support. In those days we didn't have a credit card, and Penny knew that if the person making the appeal that night was even mildly effective, I would probably put my hand in my pocket and give all the cash we had, regardless of the need to buy petrol and food on the way home. And my primary motivation would be guilt. Hence the blazing row as we prepared to go in and worship.

I don't remember how we resolved our argument that night, but I do remember one thing. I decided it was about time I found out what the Bible really taught about giving. That decision was the first step on a long journey. A journey that took me deep into the Bible, and taught me so much that I ended up teaching others. Teaching others in the local church led to me teaching seminars in a Christian conference, and after one of those seminars a friend gently but firmly told me I should put it all in a book. So here we are. I invite you to join me on the journey.

The very first thing I discovered in my journey through the Bible is that God himself is the greatest giver of all time. All we can ever learn about giving, we learn from God. *"God loved the world so much that he GAVE his only son..."* (Jn 3:16). God expresses his love by giving. He gave of himself and he gave his Son, who in turn gave his life that we might live. Giving is an expression of love. It is possible to give without loving, but the fact is that we cannot love without giving. Quite simply, it is in the very nature of God to give. It hit me the moment I turned to the opening chapter of Genesis.

In the beginning God created the heavens and the earth. The earth was formless and empty. But God gave it shape and then filled it with abundance. He gave of himself; he spoke words of life, and poured all his creative energies into this wonderful breath-taking creation. At the end of his creative work, God sat back in satisfaction and saw that all that he had made was good. In fact, it was very good. Filled to overflowing with colour, variety, beauty, intricate detail, and incredible harmony. Old Testament scholar Walter Brueggemann describes God's creative generosity in these terms: "The Bible starts out with a liturgy of abundance. Genesis chapter one is a song of praise for God's generosity [...] It declares that God blesses, that is, endows with vitality [...] And it pictures the creator as saying, "Be fruitful and multiply. In an orgy of fruitfulness everything in its kind is to multiply the overflowing goodness that pours from God's creator spirit."[1]

What Brueggemann calls this liturgy of abundance is not confined to the living things that grow and multiply and bear fruit. The stars in the sky are an amazing example of God's sheer generosity. Scientists vary in their estimates of the number of stars in the Universe. They used to be measured in millions, now they're measured in billions, and some even talk about trillions. In a throwaway line in Genesis, the writer tells us, "He also made the stars."

God was not mean with his stars. In fact, he's not mean with anything. His generosity and abundance are almost frightening. Neither is God's generosity restricted to his creative work. What God creates, he also provides for: with the same generosity with which it was created. Having created man in his image, we read,

"Then God said, "I give you every seed-bearing plant on the face of the whole earth and every tree that has fruit with seed in it. They will be yours for food. And to all the beasts of the earth and all the birds in the sky and all the creatures that move along the ground — everything that has the breath of life in it — I give every green plant for food. 'And it was so." (Gen 1: 29,30)

This revelation of a God who loves to give is continued throughout the Bible. Life itself is a gift from God, freely given to each one of us. That life is part of the essence of God which he imparts to us

1   Walter Brueggemann, *'The Liturgy of Abundance'*- article in the Christian Century, March 1999

through his Spirit. Gen 2 v7 says, *"The Lord God formed the man from the dust of the ground and breathed into his nostrils the breath of life, and the man became a living being."* God freely gives all that we need to sustain our life, and through the gift of love he has enabled us to reproduce. Every child born into the world is God's gift of new life. Each one unique, not a clone but made in the image of God.

As we read through the Bible we see also the free gift of eternal life, given in abundance to all who will receive. If Adam and Eve had eaten from the tree of life instead of the tree of knowledge of good and evil, they would have had eternal life from the beginning. But even in the face of our sin and rebellion God gives the free gift of his Son in order that we might be forgiven and receive eternal life through faith. This is grace. Abundant love which gives and gives even though we don't deserve. God's gifts are given, not earned.

God gave the whole earth to mankind and invited them to *"fill the earth and subdue it."* It was theirs as a gift from God. When God made Adam and Eve he gave them a beautiful garden in which to live; a garden so wonderful it was called Paradise. After the Fall and the covenant with Noah, God renewed his covenant with Abraham and said, *"All the land that you see I will give to you and your offspring for ever… Go, walk through the length and breadth of the land, for I am giving it to you."* (Gen 13:15, 17).

The generous giving of God is seen year in, year out, and is celebrated in Psalm 65: 9-13 as an outpouring of gratitude for the harvest. All growing things are given by God, including the conditions that enable them to grow in the first place.

"You care for the land and water it; you enrich it abundantly. The streams of God are filled with water to provide the people with grain, for so you have ordained it. You drench its furrows and level its ridges; you soften it with showers and bless its crops. You crown the year with your bounty, and your carts overflow with abundance. The grasslands of the desert overflow; the hills are clothed with

gladness. The meadows are covered with flocks and the valleys are mantled with grain; they shout for joy and sing." The account in Genesis, which Walter Brueggemann described as a liturgy of abundance and a song of praise for God's generosity, continues in the Psalms.

As we reflect on the sheer unadulterated generosity of God, think of some of the words that have been used in the verses we have looked at so far. God gives *every* seed bearing plant; he gives *all* the land that you see… for *ever; every* place where you set your foot; the streams of God are *filled*; the furrows are *drenched*; the carts overflow with *abundance*; the grasslands *overflow*. God's generosity is unparalleled, and the Old Testament records are full of this knowledge, to the point of rejoicing. Psalm 23 describes the Lord as a good shepherd looking after his sheep in every way, providing generously for their every need. *"The Lord is my shepherd, I shall not want, he makes me lie down in green pastures, he leads me beside still waters… You prepare a table before me… my cup overflows. Surely goodness and love will follow me all the days of my life."*

The Bible goes on to show that God's giving overflows into blessing. God blesses his people because he loves to give. Blessing is giving multiplied, extended and expanded almost beyond words. More often than not it is described in terms of an outpouring so generous it cannot be contained, as in Mal 3:10, *"See if I will not throw open the floodgates of heaven and pour out so much blessing you will not have room enough for it."*

The New Testament begins with the story of Christmas, still recognised today as a season of giving, despite the corruption of materialism and consumerism that marks the season of Christmas in today's society. At Christmas we are all encouraged to give generously in celebration of God's great gift of his Son, but no matter how much we may give to one another we can never out-give the God whose very nature it is to give. *"If you then, though you are evil, know how to give good gifts to your children, how much more will your Father in heaven give good gifts to those who ask him!"* (Matt 7:11).

Humanly speaking, Christmas was just the beginning of God's free gift of salvation. After God gave his Son, the Son gave his life as a free gift for your sin and mine, again as an expression of his great love. *"Greater love has no one than this, that he lay down his life for his friends."* (Jn 15:13). That gift freely given on the cross is to be freely received by faith. *"For it is by grace you have been saved, through faith – and this not from yourselves –it is the gift of God."* (Eph 2:8). The gift of God in Christ continues with the gift of the Holy Spirit, first poured out on to the church on the Day of Pentecost. The giving of God continues to be lavish and abundant, given freely to all who receive Christ. *"I will pour out my Spirit on all people, your sons and daughters will prophesy, your young men will see visions, your old men will dream dreams. Even on my servants, both men and women, I will pour out my Spirit in those days, and they will prophesy."* (Acts 2:17,18) As God the Father, Son and Holy Spirit gives himself freely to his people, so the Holy Spirit continues to give gifts, to enable us to reveal Christ to the world. There are many and varied gifts, given not earned, but there is something for everyone. *"Now to each one the manifestation of the Spirit is given for the common good."* (1 Cor 12:7)

The nature of God is to give, as an expression of his love. There is a wonderful example of this in Jesus' parable of the Workers in the Vineyard, recorded in Matt 20:1-16. The parable describes how a man went out early in the morning to hire men to work in his vineyard. They discussed payment and agreed terms. He would pay them a denarius for a day's work, which in those days could be a full twelve hours. A denarius was a fair wage for a twelve hour day. Later that day he hired other workers at different times, telling them he would pay whatever was right, and they all went to work as soon as they were taken on. Some worked for nine hours, some six, some three, and the last for just one hour. Those who only worked one hour were not lazy. They had been in the marketplace all day, looking for work. When the landowner went out at the eleventh hour and asked them why they had been standing there all day, they replied, *'Because no one has hired us.'*

At the end of the twelve hour day, the workers were all paid, beginning with those who had been hired last. Each one received a denarius, regardless of how many hours they had worked. Those who had been hired first complained because they had done twelve times more work than those hired last, yet they had all been paid the same. The owner replied,

"Friend, I am not being unfair to you. Didn't you agree to work for a denarius? Take your pay and go. I want to give the man who was hired last the same as I gave you. Don't I have the right to do what I want with my own money? Or are you envious because I am generous?"

Some people find it hard to get their heads round a situation that appears to be manifestly unfair. It's not fair; it's more than fair; it's 'fair plus'. Let's put this in a more modern context.

Penny's grandfather used to tell of his uncle, who worked in the docks in London's East End, during the Great Depression in the 1880s. He and hundreds of other men would arrive early at the dockyard gates, desperate for work. Every day only a fraction of those present would be taken on. The others had to face another day without work and without income, which often meant themselves and their families going without food. The next day they would be there again, hoping that this time perhaps they might be one of the lucky ones taken on.

Imagine in that situation a big hearted dockyard manager deciding to employ some extra men at lunchtime, and then going further and employing still more at teatime. And knowing the situation they were in, he decides to give them all a full day's pay regardless of how much work they've done. Is that unfair? And if it is, is that more than fair or less than fair? I rather think in that situation that those who had been working all day would not be complaining of unfairness. They would be grateful that they were one of the lucky ones who had found work, and they might even be grateful to the kind manager for treating their less fortunate colleagues so generously.

There are two important lessons we can learn from this parable. First, in the kingdom of heaven we will all receive the same reward, whether we have spent a lifetime serving God with all our heart, soul, mind and strength, or whether we spent a lifetime acting selfishly, and then turned to Christ on our deathbed. It may not seem fair to some, but grace goes beyond what is fair. Grace is 'fair plus'.

The second lesson is that the vineyard owner, who represents God, wants to be generous. He goes beyond the normal limitations of fairness so that he can be generous even when that generosity has not been earned or deserved. It's called grace. Here is God being generous not because someone's earned or deserved it; but simply because he wants to be generous. It's his nature. God loves to give, and when he gives he loves to give generously. He could have given more to those who had worked hard all day, but they hadn't trusted his generosity, and had struck a bargain with him, which they expected him to stick to. Until, that is, he turned out to be more generous than they had anticipated!

God is more than fair. He wants to give. He wants to be generous. And the reason I'm pressing this point is that he wants us to be the same. He wants us to be generous and big hearted, even when that means being 'more than fair'. Jesus made this clear in his teaching in the Sermon on the Mount. *"And if someone wants to sue you and take your tunic, let him have your cloak as well. If someone forces you to go one mile, go with him two miles. Give to the one who asks you, and do not turn away from the one who wants to borrow from you."* (Matt 5:40-42)

Now that's really unfair! That blows fairness out of the water. Looking ahead, if we want to learn to give as Jesus wants us to give, then we need to go beyond tithing. Tithing is fair. It's the same proportion for everyone; it takes account of our different circumstances; and it's especially fair when God promises to look after us if our tithing leaves us a bit short. But Jesus calls us to go beyond tithing, and even beyond what's fair. He calls us to go the second mile, and what's more he calls us to do so willingly and cheerfully.

Is that possible for you? Could you be generous? Is it such a big ask? I'm sure we can all think of someone we know who is generous and big hearted by nature. Stop and think for a moment. Name someone you could describe in that way. Do those people go through life heavy and burdened because they have the misfortune of being generous, or do they actually seem to enjoy being that way? Wouldn't you love to be like that?

Having begun with the God who gives, even of himself, the New Testament ends with the promise that the generous giving of God will last for eternity. *"Behold I am coming soon! My reward is with me, and I will give to everyone according to what he has done... Whoever is thirsty, let him come; and whoever wishes; let him take the free gift of the water of life."* (Rev 22:12 & 17).

It is simply not in God's nature to be mean or stingy. In a world where there is so much suffering and pain, and where even Christians sometimes doubt whether God is really interested in our wellbeing, it is crucially important to know in our hearts that God is a loving father who loves to bless his children. One of the real and lasting benefits of what came to be known as the Toronto Blessing in the mid 1990s[2] was the deeper realisation and appreciation of the Father's love, and his heart of compassion for all people.

---

2   Guy Chevreau, *'Catch the Fire'*. HarperCollins: London. 1994

In some churches it is common for the preacher to declare: "God is good!" to which the congregation responds, "All the time!" This may seem simplistic and banal to some, but the sentiment is true, and every Christian needs to grasp hold of this truth. God is good and he is generous with his love. His nature is such that he simply loves to give to his children and bless them. If ever there was a good father, his name is God. The following story is a tiny illustration of his goodness, but at the time it had a huge impact on Penny and myself.

As a ministerial student I was often sent out to nearby Baptist churches to preach and lead services, as part of my training. One Sunday after leading both the morning and evening service in the same church, a lady came up to me carrying a large white box. She looked at me with a degree of uncertainty and asked if I had any family. When I replied that I had a wife and four children, she said, "Oh that's good. I ice cakes for competitions and I felt the Lord prompting me this morning to give you this cake. It's rather a large cake and I thought it would be too much for you on your own, but now I know you've got four children I feel happy about giving it to you."

When I arrived home with this large box, Penny had just finished putting the children to bed, and was feeling tired and low. Life was a bit of a struggle and financially things were very tight. She didn't mind that for herself, but felt it was hard for the kids. That very day she had asked God for something nice for the children. When we opened the box we discovered the biggest and most beautifully iced chocolate cake we had ever seen. I was gobsmacked, and Penny was in tears. We discovered later that it tasted as good as it looked!

That was one very small example of God's amazing capacity to provide for our needs. We had a bigger illustration when God provided a house for our first ministry in Broad Haven.

2 God Gives a House

In 1988, as I came to the end of my ministerial training in Cardiff, I received an invitation to pastor a small Baptist church in Broad Haven, Pembrokeshire. We felt very much that God was leading us, and Penny and I were excited about the move. There was however one small problem. We had four children but the church had no manse. We did have a mortgage on a small bungalow in Saundersfoot, and we assumed that once we had sold it we would be able to buy somewhere suitable in Broad Haven.

The spring of 1988 saw a dramatic boom in the housing market. For some reason houses started selling like hot cakes and house prices rose higher and higher. The church at Broad Haven kept us informed whenever a likely looking house came on the market, but they were selling so fast that when we travelled down from Cardiff to look at a house, it was often sold before we had a chance to make an offer. Spring blossomed into summer, and I was busy studying for my final exams. The induction date was set for July 16th and there was still no sign of a house.

Then one evening during a time of prayer at our housegroup in Cardiff, a remarkable thing happened. We had asked the group to pray for our housing situation as we were beginning to get anxious. One of the group who had never been to Broad Haven had a vision of a house. She felt God saying this house was for us. She described it as the sort of house a child would draw. A detached house with a door in the middle, a window either side and three windows above. There was a light oak front door, apple trees in the garden, and a stream flowing nearby. At the time we weren't aware of a stream in Broad Haven, but we were greatly encouraged, believing God had a house prepared for us when the time was right.

Nothing suitable came on the market and for the first month at Broad Haven we lived in the Church Secretary's house while he and his family were on their summer holiday. At the beginning of September we were able to move into a winter let for the next six months. It was about that time we realised that a house right opposite the church actually fitted most of the details of the vision. The front door was the wrong colour and there was no stream alongside, but there was a stream that ran under a culvert on the other side of the road. The house had been on the market earlier in the year, and we had been interested, but it was sold before the church gave us the call. We took a photograph of the house and sent it back to Cardiff via a friend, asking that she show the photograph to the lady who saw the vision, without saying anything about us, or Broad Haven.

So it was that one Sunday morning after church the lady was handed a brown paper envelope with the photograph inside. Apparently when she took out the photograph she went weak at the knees and sat down. "That's the house I saw in the vision," she said. "The door's the wrong colour, but it's the same house!"

It wasn't long before I called in on the new owners under the pretence of a "pastoral visit". I told them that we had been interested in the house when it was on the market, and the new owners kindly showed me around. It was an old house with four good sized bedrooms, a huge bathroom, a big farmhouse style kitchen, two extra rooms downstairs, a double garage, a large garden, and a small orchard complete with half a dozen apple trees. Considering our background and size of family it was perfect, except for one thing. Someone else had just bought it! Another worry was whether we would ever be able to afford it. The new owners seemed to be in the habit of buying old houses and doing them up. The kitchen had already been refitted with handmade wooden cabinets and a new oil fired Rayburn costing a few thousand pounds had been installed.

Penny remembered the apple blossom in the vision. "Apple blossom comes in the spring!" she said, "Perhaps they might decide to sell in the spring?" It did seem like wishful thinking. Spring came and went and the new owners seemed happily settled. Our winter let turned into a permanent let and our immediate accommodation needs were being met. A year went by and some of the congregation began to ask when we were going to buy our own house. Thankfully I had the faith to stand up in the pulpit one day and tell the congregation about the vision. I couldn't tell them which house it was because it wasn't fair on the owners, but I made it clear that God had shown us which house we were going to have, and it was just a matter of waiting on God's timing. I think most of the congregation thought I was naive, but they humoured me!

In the meantime the rising house prices had benefited us: we had sold the bungalow and made more than £20,000 profit. In those days that meant we had a good start towards affording our own house. Time went on, and in the summer of 1989 something quite extraordinary happened. Penny had been down to pick up the children from school, and she came rushing back, bursting with excitement. "Guess what," she said, "They've changed the front door on the house. And now it's light oak, exactly the same as the vision!" We had a job to believe what was happening, but still we had to wait. Summer turned into autumn, winter came and went, and then it was spring 1990. The apple blossom had appeared on the trees.

And then it happened. The owner of the house stopped me in the street one day and announced that they had finished doing the house up and they were ready to sell and move on. She remembered I had been interested in the house previously and wondered if I was still interested in buying. If I was, she would be happy to give me first refusal as it would save her paying for estate agents. Was I interested? I couldn't wait to get back to Penny and tell her the good news. Fortunately Penny's parents had already given us a substantial amount towards buying a house, and we had the £20,000 profit from selling the bungalow, so we felt we were able to make a reasonable offer on "our" house.

The very next day I made the offer. Having totalled our assets, and calculated the level of mortgage I thought we could afford, I offered £60,000. Two years previously before house prices had risen, the same house had been on the market for £49,500, so I thought this was a reasonable offer. Unfortunately the owners didn't agree. They had already worked out a price to cover the improvements they had made on the house, and they were asking £70,000, which meant I was £10,000 short. I was a bit taken aback by that, but I said I would go home and consider things.

Back home I worked out the figures again, and decided we might be able to stretch our offer to £65,000. Still the owners weren't happy. They had decided on the price they wanted, and they didn't want to haggle. If I couldn't match their price then they would go to the estate agents and put the property on the market. Not knowing what else to do I arranged for an estate agent to provide a valuation on the property. He valued it at £75,000. No-one could say the owners were asking too much.

This was not supposed to be happening. After waiting on the vision for nearly two years, surely God wasn't going to allow us to lose the house for lack of money? At this point I asked to meet with the deacons. I explained the situation, told them which house we were looking at, and asked if there was any possibility of the church giving us a loan. The deacons were a good bunch of people and they genuinely wanted to help, but the truth was that the church had no money in reserve. The congregation had made a valiant effort to double the offering in order to pay my stipend, but in terms of reserves the cupboard was bare. But they had faith. "Bring this to the prayer meeting on Monday," they said, "We will place it in God's hands and see what he does."

I have to say that by this time my own faith was beginning to waiver. I sat down and looked again at our finances and realised that if I was honest, we couldn't really afford the extra five thousand pounds I had offered. I had said to the deacons that we needed another five thousand pounds, but in reality we needed ten. How could I tell them that on Monday? At this point both Penny and I were in the pit of despair. We had waited so long. When the front door had been changed the previous year we had been so encouraged, but now it seemed beyond our reach. We had no more money, the church had no money, family had already helped more than we had expected. Where else could we go? Where else but God?

Without realising it, and I can only say this in hindsight, we were back where we'd been so often before. Needing to let go. God was asking us to let go of this one thing that had now become more precious to us than anything else. In desperation and tears we came before God and handed it over. "Lord," we said, "You know how much this house means to us. We really believe you want us to have it. But we don't have the money and we can't get the money. We're giving it up to you. If you want us to have this house then you will have to provide, because we can't." I won't pretend that we prayed that prayer with any great faith. It was more a case of desperation and despair.

That weekend we were really down in the dumps. I wasn't looking forward to preaching on Sunday, and I was dreading having to tell the deacons that I had miscalculated the amount and we actually needed another ten thousand pounds, not five. Five might have been possible somehow, but ten seemed completely beyond reach. To take our minds off things we went to see some old friends. They didn't know the story and we poured it all out. Sometimes it's good to have friends that are outside the situation, and we just let it all hang out, the way you can only do with close friends.

We came to the end of the story, and we all stopped for a cup of tea. And then they said something that took us completely by surprise. "That's an amazing story," they said. "We believe God really wants you to have that house. We will give you £10,000 so you can buy it." I was nonplussed. These were not wealthy people. I had never for one moment thought of asking them for money. I had simply needed someone to whom we could talk and share our despair. "We couldn't pay you back," I said. "We can only just afford the mortgage as it is." "No," they said, "We're not talking about a loan. We want to give you a gift. God wants you to have this house and we believe God wants us to give you the money."

I don't remember how long we tried to resist, but they were adamant that this was what God wanted them to do, and eventually we said yes. On the Monday morning I arranged to see the owner, and offered her the asking price of £70,000. We agreed the deal and shook hands on it. That evening at the prayer meeting I have to say I was a bit naughty. A large group of people squeezed into our small vestry with sober faces, prepared to do some serious praying. "Before we pray," I said, "Let me just remind you of how this all began." I told the whole story again, as not everyone was aware of the details, and then to their astonishment told them what had happened over the weekend, and how I had shaken hands on the deal that very morning.

Some of those present could hardly believe what they had just heard. They were so grateful that I had spoken about the vision from the pulpit, some twelve months earlier. "If you hadn't done that," they said, "We would have thought you were making the whole thing up." I can still remember Peter, one of our deacons saying, "This is unreal. It's the sort of thing you read about in books!"

On November 6th, 1990, we moved into the house that God had provided. We had popped in the night before to do a few jobs and there were fireworks going off all over the place. Other people were celebrating Bonfire Night, but we were celebrating the goodness of our God! The house was finally ours, two and a half years after our friend in Cardiff had first seen the vision. Our fifth child had been born just six months before we moved in, and we and our five children lived in that house for the next 20 years, from 1990 to 2010, when God called us to a new ministry in Breconshire.

Reflecting on this story of God's amazing grace, we learn three important lessons: about letting go; about giving; and about God himself. In terms of letting go, there are times in life when God calls us to let go of the one thing that has become more important to us than anything else. Sometimes the thing that has become so important to us is in danger of taking God's place in our lives. It is for this very reason that God will often bring us to a point where we have to 'let go' of whatever it is, and simply trust God. And if the Lord tells us to let go and hand it over, then let go we must. ✗

Second, we learned that when God wants to give, he relies on people to be the channel for his love and grace. It was obvious that our friends were prompted by God to give the £10,000, and it was extremely generous of them to do so. But before the generosity came obedience. They could have said no to God's prompting. And if they had said no to God, then the following 20 years of wonderful blessing would never have happened. Our giving can be a wonderful channel for God's love, grace and blessing. If the provision of the house taught me that God loves to give, it also taught me that God gives through people.

Third, we learned that God is good. That may seem obvious, but in my years as a minister I have learned that many Christians struggle with this basic concept. So often I come across people who believe that as Christians they should expect sacrifice and self-denial and just accept that life will always be less than it could be. Sacrifice and self-denial are certainly part of the Christian lifestyle, but that doesn't alter the fact that God is good. He does actually know the desires of our hearts and he wants to bless us. The house was perfect for Penny and I, and not just because it was large enough for the whole family. Penny and I both love old houses, partly because I was brought up in a 300 year old farmhouse, and this was the house of our dreams. God knew how we'd feel about the house before we even set eyes on it, and he chose to bless us.

God gives with generous love, and we can learn to do the same. That's what this book is all about. But first we need to grapple with a few home truths about human nature.

3 Taker and Keepers

In the film, '3:10 to Yuma' [3], Russell Crowe plays the part of Ben Wade, an outlaw in the Wild West of the late 1800s. Wade is captured by a posse of lawmen, one of whom decides to take the outlaw's fine looking horse for himself. During the night, despite being handcuffed, Wade manages to grab a knife and stabs the lawman to death. In his defence he calmly says, "He took my horse." "That doesn't give you the right to take his life!" shouts the Sheriff. Wade narrows his eyes and expresses a truth that has been evident throughout history. "It's man's nature to take what he wants – that's how we're born."

It is the nature of God to give, and the nature of man to take. This was my conclusion after reading the first two chapters of Genesis. With my Bible open in front of me, I saw a stark difference between page two and page three. On page two I encountered the very first reference in the Bible to giving. God said, "*I give you every seed-bearing plant on the face of the whole earth and every tree that has fruit with seed in it*" (Gen 1:29). Then on page three I read the first reference to taking. Having been commanded by God not to eat of the tree of the knowledge of good and evil, Eve, tempted by Satan, reached out her hand, took what did not belong to her, and ate it. Sin entered into the human heart, human nature was corrupted, and mankind, made in the image

---

3   '*3:10 to YUMA*', directed by James Mangold, Lionsgate 2007

of the God who loves to give, became takers. The hand that was created to give closed into a fist.

When Eve reached out her hand and took what did not belong to her, she started a trend. The Old Testament is full of "takers". When Cain sees that God approves of Abel's offering, but not his own, he takes his brother's life and commits the first murder in history. Jacob, one of twins, is born grasping his brother's heel, and is known as a grasper for the rest of his life. He takes his brother's birth right and then tricks his brother out of his father's blessing. In his grandfather Abraham's time, King Abimelech sees that Abraham's wife, Sarah, is beautiful, and it says in Gen 20:2 that he simply sent for her and took her.

It seems strange that kings, of all people, would be tempted to take anything from anyone. You would think that any self-respecting king in those days would have plenty of their own. But that is precisely the point. Mankind has a tendency to take, not because they need to, but simply because it's in their nature. The more they have, the more they want. The more they get, the more they take.

When the Israelites first asked for a king, Samuel prophesied that their kings would be takers. Until then, God had reigned over them through his prophets, but the Israelites decided they wanted a king like the other nations around them. Samuel felt rejected and angry, but the Lord told him not to take it personally. It was not Samuel the people were rejecting, but God. As they wanted a human king rather than a divine king, God warned them through Samuel how a human king would treat them.

"He will take your sons and make them serve with his chariots... He will take your daughters to be perfumers and cooks and bakers... He will take the best of your fields and vineyards... He will take a tenth of your grain and your wine... He will take your menservants and maidservants... He will take a tenth of your flocks and you yourselves will become his slaves." (1 Sam 8:11-17)

The story of King David in 2 Samuel 11 is a clear example of this. David is on the roof of his palace one evening when he looks down and sees another man's wife taking a bath. Despite the fact that the woman's husband Uriah is one of David's loyal soldiers, risking his life at that very moment in a military campaign, David sends for the woman and takes what does not belong to him. Having taken hold of Bathsheba, he then wants to keep her for himself, and so he arranges for her husband to be murdered. Cynically, he arranges for Uriah's death to look as though it were just a normal casualty of battle. Nathan the prophet graphically illustrates what David has done by telling the story of a rich man who has flocks in abundance but callously takes a poor man's only lamb to feed a visiting friend.

One of the frightening aspects of this story is that King David is that same David referred to in 1 Sam 13:14, where it says that, *"The Lord has sought out a man after his own heart."* Even those close to God have a tendency to take and keep, because it is in the very nature of fallen mankind.

Old Testament kings certainly have a bad record in this respect. One of the worst examples is the story of Naboth's vineyard in 1 Kings 21. King Ahab of Samaria decides that Naboth's vineyard, next door to the king's palace, would be a handy place for a vegetable garden. The King has plenty of money and offers to buy the vineyard outright, or exchange it for a better one elsewhere. But Naboth declines the offer and refuses to sell. The vineyard is part of his family inheritance and it means a lot to him. The matter should have ended there. The king might have been a bit peeved about his offer being refused, but surely acquiring a vegetable garden next to the palace wasn't the most important item on the king's agenda?

What happens next is almost unbelievable. The king of Samaria acts like a little boy, sulking and throwing a tantrum because he can't get what he wants. I once referred to this story in a school assembly, and the teachers couldn't believe that such an accurate portrayal of a sulking child existed in the Bible! Verse 4 says that King Ahab *"...went home, sullen and angry... He lay on his bed sulking and refused to eat."* His wife Jezebel, after scolding him for his petty behaviour, promises to get him what he wants. Jezebel arranges for Naboth to be slandered. He is accused by 'witnesses' of cursing the king, and is subsequently stoned to death. As soon as King Ahab hears the news, he promptly gets up from his sulking, and takes possession of Naboth's vineyard.

This natural tendency to take often resulted in serious consequences, none more so than in the story of Achan, recorded in Joshua 6 and 7. After the Israelites had marched for seven days around Jericho, they gave a great shout and the walls collapsed. Before the soldiers charged in to capture the city, Joshua warned them that God had specifically commanded that no-one should take any articles of gold or silver for themselves. With stern words he warned them that if they did so they would bring trouble on the nation, and destruction on themselves. But fallen human nature is hard to resist. An Israelite soldier called Achan could not resist taking a beautiful robe, two hundred shekels of silver, and fifty shekels of gold.

After the spectacular victory at Jericho, the Israelites thought the capture of the next city would be a piece of cake. They sent a small force of two or three thousand men, but were dismayed when they were soundly defeated. Joshua tore his clothes and cried out to God, who told him that someone in the camp had disobeyed his orders and taken plunder for themselves. Eventually Achan was found out and he confessed saying, *"I coveted them and took them. They are hidden in the ground inside my tent."* (Joshua 7:21). The punishment was severe. Achan and his family, his animals and possessions were stoned and burned, in a valley called 'Achor' - the valley of destruction. The entry of the people into the Promised Land was meant to be a new start for Israel, living under the laws of God, but their tendency to take was still ingrained in their fallen human nature.

If the Old Testament seems full of 'takers', the emphasis in the New Testament is more focussed on 'keepers'. A clear and graphic example is found in the story of the rich young man, recorded in Mark 10:17-25.

Imagine the scene. A hot dusty day in a small village in Judea. Jesus and his disciples are passing through a village on their way to Jerusalem. Word spreads quickly. "The teacher from Nazareth is here!" Excited crowds. Anticipation. A sense of expectancy.

A young man falls on his knees before Jesus and asks how he can inherit eternal life. In the conversation that follows it becomes clear that the man is sincere, and that his one desire is to please God. Mark records that *"Jesus looked at him and loved him."* After a brief conversation Jesus says, *"Come, follow me."*

What an invitation! Jesus is inviting him to join the Twelve – to go wherever Jesus goes; to follow him; to be with him; to learn from him; to be one of his disciples. One day his story will be immortalised in the Gospels of Matthew, Mark and Luke. They will all record the same thing - he refused to follow Jesus. He couldn't do it because there was something in his life more important than God. Jesus challenged him to let go. To give it up. To put God first in his life. But he couldn't let go. He was a 'keeper'.

Many years later, writing his Gospel, Mark remembered that day with sadness. The incident in the little village on the way to Jerusalem. The crowd, the noise, the dust, the hubbub all around. The moment that young man fell on his knees before Jesus. He was genuinely sincere. He would have made a good disciple. Perhaps even an Apostle. With a sigh Mark wrote, *"Jesus looked at him and loved him. 'One thing you lack' he said. 'Go, sell everything you have and give to the poor. Then come, follow me.' At this the man's face fell. He went away sad, because he had great wealth."*

He walked away from Jesus. The cost was too great. He'd always had money; it was his security; his future. And he couldn't let go. Jesus knew this rich young man was not alone in his dilemma, and said, *"How hard it is for the rich to enter the kingdom of God… it is easier for a camel to enter through the eye of a needle than for a rich man to enter the kingdom of God."*

Why is it so hard for the rich to enter the kingdom of God? Because the more we have, the greater the desire to keep, and the harder it is to let go. The more we have, the more tempting it is to put our security in what we have; a temptation that isn't particularly appealing to the poor. When Jesus commended the poor widow for putting two small copper coins into the temple treasury, she was in effect doing what the rich young man failed to do. She was giving all she had. But somehow, when all you have in the world is two small copper coins, there isn't the same temptation to put your security in what you have. In that situation, it's actually easier to put your security in God. Not so for the rich. When you have a fine home, a good income and plenty of savings, it's very tempting indeed to put your security in what you have. It's very tempting to hold on to what you have, to keep it, and make sure you don't lose it.

The story of the rich fool in Luke 12 is another example of someone holding on to what he has, and eventually losing everything. This rich farmer has such a good harvest that he runs out of room to store all his grain. An opportunity to give some of it away to the poor, perhaps? Or perhaps not.

"This is what I'll do. I will tear down my barns and build bigger ones, and there I will store all my grain and goods. And I'll say to myself… Take life easy; eat, drink and be merry. But God said to him, 'You fool! This very night your life will be demanded from you. Then who will get what you have prepared for yourself?' This is how it will be with anyone who stores up things for himself but is not rich towards God."

If we're honest, many of us will recognise a similar attitude in our churches. How often does a church receive an unexpected legacy and respond by storing it away for a 'rainy day' rather than giving it to the poor or using it to further the mission of the church? Why? Because suddenly we see the possibility of ensuring we have some financial security for the future. The tendency to keep is as strong today as it ever was.

The story of Ananias and Sapphira in Acts 5 makes even more uncomfortable reading. In those heady days of the early church, many Christians were so filled with the Spirit that they were giving land and houses to the poor. It would seem that Ananias and Sapphira wanted to do the same, but it was hard to resist the tendency of their fallen nature. Selling a piece of property, Ananias brought the money to the Apostles and laid it at their feet. He stated that he was giving all the money from the sale to the poor, but *"With his wife's full knowledge he kept back part of the money for himself."* You would think that he was being pretty generous anyway, having sold property and given some of the money to the poor, but look how God responds. He causes Ananias to fall down dead. When questioned, his wife Sapphira insists that this was all the money, and she too falls down dead. It would seem that in the context of the new church being renewed in the image of its creator, God was not going to allow the old nature of 'taking and keeping' to rear its ugly head in the church.

The next example shows that this tendency to take and keep can just as easily affect Christian leaders. When Mary anoints the feet of Jesus with expensive perfume, Judas, one of the Twelve, reacts indignantly. *"Why wasn't this perfume sold and the money given to the poor?' He did not say this because he cared about the poor but because he was a thief; as keeper of the money bag, he used to help himself to what was put into it."* (Jn 12:5,6). What really made Judas indignant was Mary's extravagant generosity. Those who hoard and keep are made uncomfortable by generous giving. To them it is an anathema.

Why is there a difference between the Old and New Testament, with the emphasis in regard to man's nature taking a subtle shift from taking to keeping? Is it perhaps that as time went on money itself became a greater and more common factor? In the Old Testament they tithed their animals and crops, but by the time of the New Testament money was in more common use. Money is a strange thing. In one sense paper money has no real value whatsoever, yet it represents something valuable, and is easily hoarded. As such it is very easy to place our security in how much money we have, be it in the bank or under the mattress. Once we start to place our trust and security in money, it can very easily take the place of God. Which is why Jesus said, "*Do not store up for yourselves treasures on earth... for where your treasure is, there your heart will be also... No one can serve two masters... You cannot serve both God and money.*" (Matt 6:19-24).

The big challenge is to let go – to let go of our money, and put God in his rightful place. Letting go is a huge challenge, one that I've had to face up to again and again in my own life. In my school days I heard a legend about a particular tribe of natives who devised a novel way of catching wild monkeys. They would fix a heavy clay pot to the ground, somewhere out in the forest, and half fill it with peanuts. They would then retire a suitable distance and await developments. Before long a wild monkey would smell the peanuts and come to investigate. The monkey would find that the neck of the pot was just wide enough for him to squeeze his hand down into the pot, where he would take hold of a fistful of peanuts. Unfortunately the neck of the clay pot wasn't wide enough for him to retrieve a full fist. Unwilling to let go of his prize, and not strong enough to lift the pot, the monkey found his hand was trapped and would soon become very agitated. He would jump up and down and screech in anger, attracting the attention of the nearby natives. As his captors approached, the monkey would sense the danger and become even more agitated, but nothing would make him let go of the peanuts. His desire to hold on to what was in his hand overcame his natural sense of self preservation, and the hunters would catch him with a net while he was still jumping up and down, screeching with indignation and refusing to let go of his prize. There are times in life when it's really hard to let go.

Sometimes it's the small things in life that teach us the big lessons. The following example of my own letting go was such a small thing, and yet my struggle was very similar to our friend the monkey.

As part of our ministerial training we were often sent out on a Sunday to lead services in local chapels. One particular Sunday morning I was heading up the A470 from Cardiff, in a bit of a hurry as I'd allowed only just enough time to get to the chapel, when I discovered to my horror that I'd left something behind. As part of my children's talk I was going to give away a packet of Smarties, and I suddenly realised I'd left them on the kitchen table. I didn't have time to go back for them, and in those days there were no shops open on a Sunday morning. I had very few children's talks in my limited repertoire, and without the necessary props there was nothing else I could do.

The point of giving away the Smarties was simply to illustrate the Gospel. I would ask if anyone wanted some Smarties, and then say that all they had to do was to come forward and ask. If they asked they would receive, as with the Gospel. As I didn't have any Smarties, I would have to find something else that would be tempting enough to persuade a young child to come forward and ask. Still driving with one hand, I frantically began to search the car for any suitable alternatives.

There was nothing in the glove compartment... nothing in the side door pocket... nothing on the back seat... nothing in my jacket pocket... except for a rather nice Parker pen which my brother had given me for my birthday.

Then began a rather uncomfortable conversation with God. I must have been mistaken, but for a moment I thought he was saying I should give away my pen. A ridiculous idea, of course. It was my birthday present. I continued searching the car with my spare hand, but there was nothing remotely suitable. Apart from the pen.

"No way." I thought. "Not my pen."

"Why not?" said God.

"Well… it's a Parker. My birthday present… My brother would be offended."

"Would he?"

"Well… if he wasn't offended, I still wouldn't want to give it."

"Why not?"

"Because it's my pen."

"You mean it's yours."

"That's right. It's mine."

"I thought you said once that everything that's yours is mine?"

"Well yes. But that doesn't mean I have to give my pen. Does it?"

"Give them the pen, Ifor."

"But I don't want to. It's mine."

"Give them the pen."

I won't bore you with the rest, but when I finally said 'Yes' to God, it was through gritted teeth and with very little grace. Prompted partly by the fact that I was desperate, and I just couldn't think of anything else to give.

When it came to the children's talk, I held up my shiny Parker pen, and told the children that if anyone wanted it, all they had to do was come and ask. Part of me hoped that no-one would move.

Unfortunately one little girl came eagerly to the front and asked for my pen. "There you are," I said, "Now it's yours for keeps. Simply because you asked. It's like that with Jesus."

On the way home I was not a happy bunny, and for a little while if I'm honest, God was not my favourite person. In fact, if I'm really honest, I sulked for days. And then on the Thursday morning I had a letter from the church secretary.

"Dear Mr Williams," she wrote. "Thank you for the service on Sunday morning, and thank you for giving your pen to little Sarah. She took it in to school to show her teacher, and she's very proud of it."

"I bet she is," I thought, as I continued reading.

"I thought it was so good of you to give her your pen, and I wanted to give you something in return. Please accept the enclosed with my thanks."

The enclosed was a long thin box. Inside was a Parker pen, exactly the same colour and model as the one I'd given away, but brand new! I sat there and cried. God had told me to give away a pen. It was only a pen, but who knows the effect that simple illustration may have had on someone sitting in the congregation, believing in Jesus but not knowing how to become a Christian. And there was I, arguing with God about letting go of a pen! And what's more, our gracious, patient God had even taken the trouble to teach me a lesson about God providing. The lesson that whatever we give, we can never out give God.

It was only a little thing, but I learnt an awful lot that day about our natural desire to hold on to what we have, and the need to obey God when he prompts us to let go. Letting go is a sacrifice, and sacrifice was one of the first lessons that God's people had to learn.

PART 2

GOD TEACHES GIVING WITH AN OPEN HAND

4 When Worship Meant Sacrifice

W hen we think of Old Testament worship, we normally think of sacrifice. In Genesis 4 we find the very first mention of mankind bringing an offering to God. Cain and Abel each bring a spontaneous offering of worship, and the offering takes the form of a sacrifice. In the early days people like Abraham, Isaac and Jacob would build an altar with their bare hands, usually in a place where they had encountered God in a significant way, and there on the altar they would worship with a sacrifice. In time, what started as a spontaneous act of worship became established in Old Testament Law as a permanent command.

When the Israelites became a nation in their own right and wandered for forty years in the desert, God commanded them to build a portable Tent of Meeting, or Tabernacle, where all offerings of worship could be sacrificed on the one altar dedicated to God. After the Israelites settled in the Promised Land of Canaan, King Solomon built a permanent Temple in Jerusalem, where the whole nation would worship God by sacrificing offerings on the altar.

Initially, these sacrifices were the main way in which the people gave to God in worship. Alongside the special offerings made at particular times of the year, such as Passover and the Day of Atonement, there developed a regular sacrifice which involved the Israelites giving the first tenth of their crops as they were harvested and the firstborn of their flocks and herds. Over time, these crops and animals were exchanged for money which was used to buy items for sacrifice (Dt 14:24-26), and later still the tithe became a monetary offering given to the Temple treasury. The financial offering taken up during church services every Sunday is a natural development of this instinctive desire to give to God in worship.

The example of Cain and Abel has much to teach us about the principles of giving which were laid down in the Old Testament. *"Now Abel kept flocks, and Cain worked the soil. In the course of time Cain brought some of the fruits of the soil as an offering to the Lord. But Abel brought fat portions from some of the firstborn of his flock. The Lord looked with favour on Abel and his offering, but on Cain and his offering he did not look with favour."* (Gen 4:2-5)

First we see that one offering was acceptable to God, whilst the other was not. That theme is developed throughout the Bible story. When sacrificial offerings were regulated in Old Testament Law, they had to be offered in accordance with strict criteria if they were to be accepted. So for instance, we read, *"If the offering is a burnt offering from the herd, he is to offer a male without defect. He must present it at the entrance to the Tent of Meeting so that it will be acceptable to the Lord."* (Lev 1 v3)

When the offering became a financial one in the form of the tithe, it became embedded in the worship of the Israelites who recognised that the tithe itself belonged to God (Lev 27:30). That offering had to be the whole tenth; anything less was unacceptable. When the Israelites withheld part of the tithe, God showed very clearly through the prophet Malachi that this was unacceptable, to the extent that he accused them of robbing God. *"Will a man rob God? Yet you rob me." But you ask, 'How do we rob you?' 'In tithes and offerings. You are under a curse - the whole nation of you - because you are robbing me. Bring the whole tithe into the storehouse, that there may be food in my house."* (Mal 3:8-10)

This theme of acceptable sacrifice is developed in the New Testament. The male lamb without defect becomes the sinless Lamb of God, the Son of God called Jesus, who came to save his people from their sin by offering up his life as the only sacrifice acceptable to God. A remarkable but little known link in this chain comes in the Old Testament sacrifice made on the annual Day of Atonement. First we have an example of sacrifice which is not acceptable, when Aaron's sons, Nadab and Abihu, fill their censers with fire and incense and offer *"unauthorised fire before the Lord, contrary to his command. So fire came out from the presence of the Lord and consumed them, and they died before the Lord."* (Lev 10:1,2)

Later, on the Day of Atonement, in contrast to the two sons who offered unacceptable sacrifice, we read, *"The priest who is anointed and ordained to succeed his father as high priest is to make atonement. He is to put on the sacred linen garments and make atonement for the Most Holy Place, for the Tent of Meeting, and the altar, and for the priests and all the people of the community."* (Lev 16:32,33)

After all the emphasis on acceptable sacrifice in the Old Testament Law, it transpires that there was only one person who could make an acceptable sacrifice of atonement: the son who was anointed to succeed his father. This theme is later picked up by Paul, who tells the Romans that, *"God presented (his son) as a sacrifice of atonement, through faith in his blood."* (Ro 3:25). Or as John the Baptist put it, *"Behold, the Lamb of God, who takes away the sin of the world!"* (Jn 1 v29)

In Genesis 4, Abel's offering is accepted, but Cain's offering is rejected. Is that purely because of the symbolic significance of the lamb? In the Bible we often see great truths presented symbolically, but there are more immediate lessons on acceptable giving in this passage. Many people would think that Cain is being treated unfairly. It's not his fault that he has no lamb to offer; he's a farmer growing crops. But symbolism aside, it's not about what Cain and Abel gave. It's more about their attitude. It seems to me that Cain and Abel had very different attitudes to their giving. The fact that Cain brought *'some of the fruits of the soil as an offering'* suggests to me that he didn't put a lot of thought or effort into his offering. He simply brought some of what he had. Rather like the offering plate coming round in church, and people looking to see what they've got in their pocket or purse, and putting some of what they have into the plate. No great thought or sacrifice, no great offering, and certainly no great sense of worship. Abel's attitude is completely different. The contrast is marked with a 'but'. *"But Abel brought fat portions from some of the firstborn of his flock."*

The firstborn is literally just that. The lamb that was born first. The lambing season can take place over several months, which means that later on, when lambs are old enough to kill for meat, the firstborn lamb will be older and therefore bigger than the other lambs. He may in fact be twice the size of lambs born a month or two later. In other words Abel did not go to his flock and pick out any old lamb, as Cain brought some of his fruit. Abel brought the biggest, the firstborn. And having chosen his biggest lamb, he then gave the best part. Contrary to our modern tastes, in older times the fat portions of meat were considered to be by far the best. I can still remember from my youth old farmers praising the virtue of fat bacon and its ability to keep you warm on a cold day.

The fact is that when Abel brought an offering to God, he thought about it and gave the biggest and the best he had, wanting to please God with his offering. To worship God is to give him his worth; to give him the best we can, putting some thought and effort into it. It's rather like taking time to choose a birthday card or present that we know would be particularly suitable and acceptable, as opposed to picking up the first thing we see because we really can't be bothered to take time over what we're giving. A present specially chosen doesn't have to be big or expensive. Its worth is in the thought that's gone into it. Abel gave the best he could, whereas Cain gave without any great thought or effort, which is why Abel's offering was accepted and Cain's was rejected.

Giving to God is part of our worship, so we need to give him our best. That doesn't mean it has to be a large amount. Jesus commended a widow when she gave only two small copper coins, but he also showed that was all she had left in the world. It's not about the amount, it's about our attitude. In terms of attitude, it would help if, in church, we stopped talking about taking a collection and instead spoke of taking up an offering. It may be only words, but the meaning is important. The offering is part of our worship and needs to be given in an attitude of worship. This is not just about money; it extends also to the giving of ourselves to God. Paul tells us,

"Therefore I urge you brothers, in view of God's mercy, to offer your bodies as living sacrifices, holy and pleasing to God – this is your spiritual act of worship." (Ro 12:1)

So what do we learn from Cain and Abel? First we learn that giving is part of our worship. As Christians we give ourselves to God in worship, and as part of that worship we can give financially. Second, we learn that our giving may be acceptable to God, or it may not be. What counts for acceptable giving is not to do with the amount, but the attitude of our hearts. We should always seek to give God the best, even if that involves sacrifice.

Another example of sacrifice in the context of giving comes in 2 Samuel, with the story of King David and Araunah. King David has taken a census of all the soldiers of his army. It shows David's focus is on his own military strength rather than trusting in the power of God. God's anger burns against David and a plague strikes the people, causing many of them to die. The prophet Gad encourages David to show his repentance by going to the threshing floor of Araunah and offering up a sacrifice to God. David immediately went as instructed.

"Araunah said, 'Why has my lord the king come to his servant?'
'To buy your threshing floor,' David answered, 'so I can build an
altar to the Lord, that the plague on the people may be stopped.'
Araunah said to David, 'Let my lord the king take whatever pleases
him and offer it up. Here are oxen for the burnt offering, and here
are threshing sledges and ox yokes for the wood. O king, Araunah
gives all this to the king.' Araunah also said to him, 'May the Lord
your God accept you.' But the king replied to Araunah, 'No, I insist
on paying you for it. I will not sacrifice to the Lord my God burnt
offerings that cost me nothing." (2 Samuel 24:21-24)

David buys the threshing floor and the oxen for fifty shekels of
silver, builds an altar there and offers up a sacrifice of worship.
The Lord accepts the offering and the plague stops.

David's insistence on not giving to God an offering that cost him
nothing has much to say to our contemporary experience of giving
to God. So often, like Cain, we bring an offering out of what we
have in our pocket or purse, and in truth it has cost us nothing.
The only giving that counts as acceptable worship is that which
has an element of sacrifice; giving that costs.

These principles of worship and sacrifice speak to our contemporary
experience in more ways than one. When Penny and I became
Christians it was very much about worship and sacrifice.

I grew up on a farm, but had to leave home because I was one of
four brothers and there wasn't room on the farm for all of us. I left
school and went to Usk College of Agriculture with a very clear
plan. I would get an agricultural qualification, earn good money
milking cows, and one day get my own farm. Simple. A bit naïve,
but simple. I was in control and I had my future all planned out.
Then I met two people who changed everything. Penny and Jesus.

I believed in God, and so did Penny. While we were at college we
started going to the local Baptist church together and our interest
deepened. We both believed in God but neither of us had yet
made a commitment to follow Christ.

As well as growing in faith, Penny and I were also falling in love. One day she said to me, "I love you more than anyone else in the world." Or words to that effect. I must have been very pious because I replied, "That's no good. If you want to be a Christian you have to put Jesus first, not me."

Penny wasn't put off by my less than romantic response, and she decided that if she was going to give herself to anyone, she would give herself first to God. She didn't do anything religious, but one night, lying on her bed, she simply said, "Alright God. You first - Ifor second." The words were brief and to the point, but the commitment behind those words was very real. She had decided to put God first in her life. That's worship. The first of the Ten Commandments says, *"You shall have no other gods before me."* (Ex 20:3).

As she lay on her bed she began to feel what she later described as liquid peace flowing through her body from her toes right up to her head. The sensation lasted for some time and had a visible effect on her for weeks. I saw her the following morning during breakfast in the college canteen, and I said, "What's happened to you? You look so happy!" For days she felt as though she was walking on air, and though that initial feeling eventually receded, the peace of God and the joy of knowing Christ has stayed with her ever since.

Penny and I knew little if anything about the Holy Spirit in those days, but she had given herself to God, and he had given himself to her. Jesus had already died for her to be forgiven, and now he had given Penny his Spirit to dwell in her heart. I saw the difference and I wanted what she had.

In my case, however, there was a problem. I had no trouble believing in Jesus as the Son of God who died on the Cross to forgive me, and I knew I needed forgiveness. But I also knew that as well as being my Saviour, Jesus also wanted to be Lord of my life. That didn't fit with the PLAN. I had my future well and truly sorted. What if Jesus had other ideas? I battled with this for the next ten months. Penny grew and grew in her new found relationship with Jesus, and I so much wanted to be like her, but I couldn't bring myself to submit to someone else being in charge of my life.

One night we went to a meeting where I heard someone tell the story of a parachutist taking his first parachute jump. Like the others, he had been taught to pack his own parachute, and how to roll on landing in order to avoid breaking a leg. The time came for his first proper jump and he was apprehensive but looking forward to it. The others jumped out one by one, and then it was his turn. As he stood in the doorway of the aeroplane thousands of feet up in the air, suddenly everything seemed rather different. He'd never jumped out of an aeroplane before and quite frankly he was terrified. Despite all the encouragement of the assistant beside him, the would-be parachutist froze. His hands clenched the doorway of the aeroplane and nothing would make him let go. The worst thing he could do, said the speaker, would be to jump out and hold on with one hand. The result – splat!

Strangely enough, said the speaker, some people do something similar when they are in the process of becoming Christians. They want to invite Jesus to be Lord in their lives but there is something they just can't let go of. Or perhaps they decide to take that step and make a Christian commitment, but still hold on to some aspect of their lives, instead of giving it all to Jesus. The answer was simple. Let go… and let God!

Not surprisingly, that story spoke right into my situation. I knew I was refusing to let go of control. And as a result I was holding back from becoming a Christian. As the preacher said, the only way that parachute could save him was for the parachutist to let go and jump. The only way that I could receive salvation from Jesus was for me to let go of control and hand everything over to

Christ. Letting go is the modern equivalent of sacrifice. I needed to sacrifice my desire to be in control, as it was stopping me from accepting Christ as Lord.

A few days later, that's exactly what I did. Penny was with me when I decided that I couldn't resist Jesus anymore. I was ready to let go of control and ask Jesus to rule in my life, and I did that in a simple heartfelt prayer. Penny laid her hands on my head and prayed for me. As she did so, she felt something like an electric current go down her arms into my head. I felt something, but I just couldn't find the words to describe it. Initially, all I could say was that it was 'big'.

A little while later I pictured it as being like a mouse coming up against the Great Wall of China. The Great Wall is estimated to be 5,500 miles long - Land's End to John O'Groats times seven! There is no way that a mouse could begin to comprehend or express the sheer length, depth and height of the Great Wall of China. However, assuming it could talk, that mouse would be able to say. "I've been there. I've run along the wall." I felt God was saying to me, "Ifor, don't ever think you can fully understand me. You will never be able to put me in a box and say 'this is God'. But we've met. I am living inside you by my Spirit."

Worship and sacrifice. Worship is about putting God first, giving him the best. Sacrifice involves an intentional letting go of anything or anyone that might prevent us from putting God first. Sacrifice, or letting go, is essential to us learning how to give with an open hand. As takers, we need to learn to give, and as keepers, we need to learn to let go. The next two principles I found in the Old Testament were trust and obedience.

5 Trust and Obey

In 1977 I finished Agricultural College, got a job as a herdsman near Ludlow, and Penny and I were married. Three years later we moved to a farm near Leominster, and two years after that to a farm near Tenby. We still shared the dream of one day having our own farm, and we would spend hours on winter evenings trying to work out how we could one day buy a farm big enough for us to make a living. We were growing as Christians, but the dream to have our own farm was as strong as ever. It was during this time that we used some of our savings to put down a mortgage on a small bungalow in nearby Saundersfoot. We were able to let the bungalow out to holidaymakers during the summer, and the holiday income paid for the mortgage. It was all part of the grand plan to save and invest, in the hope of one day having our own farm.

In May 1984, whilst still on the farm near Tenby, we heard of a Christian ship called the LOGOS, which was paying a visit to nearby Milford Haven. The LOGOS was overseen by a mission organisation known as Operation Mobilisation, and their International Director, George Verwer, was scheduled to speak at a local meeting. It looked interesting and Penny and I decided to go along.

George Verwer is a passionate speaker, and he was encouraging people to offer themselves to serve God in one way or another. In his talk he quoted Matt 9:37, where Jesus says, *"The harvest is plentiful but the workers are few. Ask the Lord of the harvest, therefore, to send out workers into his harvest field."* That verse hit me between the eyes like a bullet. All my life the harvest had been the highlight of my year. Even as a young child when my brothers and I were too small to lift a bale of hay, we would be out in the hayfield, rolling the bales down the steep fields so that the men didn't have so far to fetch them. Then as we grew into strong young teenagers we used to pride ourselves on how hard and fast we could haul the bales. For us teenagers the hay harvest was a time of hard work, long hours, sweat and blisters, but great satisfaction and fulfilment.

Now God was speaking to me about his harvest field. I didn't hear an audible voice but I knew as clear as day that God was calling me there and then to give up farming and come and work for God in his spiritual harvest field. He was not looking for part time workers or casual labourers. He wanted me to work for God full time. When George finished his talk, my heart was burning inside me. Strangely enough, at that point there was no problem with me letting go of my lifetime's ambition to have my own farm. There was simply no competition. God had spoken and that was that. Worship means putting God first, and obedience means doing what he tells you. In that context, the sacrifice of letting go of my lifelong ambition to farm was a no-brainer.

Unfortunately, God seemed to have forgotten to say anything to Penny. She was rather taken aback to hear how God had spoken to me so clearly about giving up farming and working for God. To be fair though, after her initial shock Penny prayed about the situation and over the next few weeks became as convinced as I that God wanted us both to give up farming and work for God. There was however, one major difficulty.

As I prayed and read my bible I became convinced that God wanted us to join the LOGOS. They regularly took on volunteers for a two year period, and gave in depth training in preparation for a life time of serving God. I felt this was the ideal training and preparation for whatever specific plans God had for us in the future. The fact that we had two young children was not a problem as they had a school for children on board the ship. As the days and weeks went by I kept getting references to the sea or ships in my regular bible reading, and I was totally convinced of the next step God wanted us to take. The difficulty however was that Penny didn't see it that way at all. She had accepted that we were being called to leave farming and work for God, but she wasn't at all convinced about the ship. It seemed a lovely idea, and it would be great for the kids, but as she prayed and read her Bible she became convinced that God wanted us to work for him in Pembrokeshire. When we had first moved to Tenby with the job, she had sensed God calling us to that area, and now that sense of calling was growing ever stronger. Well of course, I knew that she had got it wrong, and she was equally sure that I had got it wrong. We argued about it, we kept quiet for a while, we came back to it, and still we were poles apart in what we felt God was saying. That was a very difficult time for us, and it lasted about three months.

Penny and I were very much in love and we did everything together. Now for the first time in seven years of marriage we just could not agree. Eventually after three months we finally agreed that for some reason we could not understand, God was telling us to go in two very different directions. She accepted that God was telling me to go on the ship for two years, and I accepted that God was telling her to stay in Pembrokeshire. One night as we discussed things in bed before we went to sleep, we made a joint decision. I would give up my job and join the ship for two years, and Penny and the children would stay behind in Pembrokeshire and live by faith. It was another 'letting go' moment, only this time we were letting go of each other in obedience to God, and trusting that somehow he would work it all out.

That night we went to sleep, at peace with God and at peace with each other, for the first time in months. The next morning it was a different story. Penny was in tears and I wasn't that happy myself. We asked our local minister to come and talk to us. We told him where we were at, and he made it clear to us that God was not in the habit of splitting up families in the way we were planning. He made me see that I was looking to the ship simply for training in Christian work. 'You don't have to go on a ship for Christian training,' he said, 'You can go as a family to Bible College.' Well that seemed to make sense and so we wrote to various Bible Colleges. Over the next few weeks we received all sorts of information through the post but none of it seemed to have that hallmark of God's calling.

One day an old friend of ours, Peter Dewi Richards, working at that time with the Bible Society, called in to see us. He actually made a huge detour because he felt that morning he had to see us. We told him the whole story and he said, "Have you thought perhaps that God might be calling you to train as a minister?" Strangely enough over the previous three months I had been so focussed on this business of two years training on board ship that I hadn't really thought of what might follow next. He talked, and we listened. After he left we turned to each other and said, "That feels right. Perhaps we should try that avenue and see what happens."

Without going into all the detail we started the process and within a short space of time we became convinced that God wanted us to move to Cardiff, where I would begin my training as a Baptist minister. Although it was wonderful to be together again in our thinking, and to be sure about this calling to the ministry, there was still a nagging doubt. I had no doubt that I was being called to the ministry, but the trouble was I had felt the same way about the LOGOS. And if I was wrong then, how could I be sure I wasn't wrong this time? I began to progress through the necessary steps, which included preaching in local churches and sharing my story of why I felt God was calling me into the ministry.

One night at a midweek prayer meeting in a local church, I had just concluded my account of the story so far, when an elderly lady approached me and gave me a completely different slant on the story. "Your story," she said, "reminds me of Abraham and Isaac in Genesis 22. God never really intended Abraham to sacrifice his son. He was simply testing Abraham to see if he would be obedient." She then proceeded to tell me how she felt it really was God telling me to go on the ship, and it really was God telling Penny to stay behind in Pembrokeshire. "I feel," she said, "That God was testing you. You've said how you are both very much together as a couple. I think God wanted to know who was really most important in your life. Was it God or Penny? For Penny, was it God or Ifor? As soon as you agreed to separate, then God was able to step in, just as he did with Abraham on the mountain. He was calling you to be a Pastor, but first you had to be tested to see whether you really would put God first, even in front of Penny."

When I heard those words, it was as though someone had switched on a light. Suddenly everything fell into place. I knew God had spoken to me about the ship, just as I later knew God was calling me to be a minister. Now at last it all fitted together. Not only was I receiving affirmation of my call to the ministry, but I was learning one of the greatest lessons in the Christian life. That if we put God first, everything else will fall into place. In the words of Jesus, *"Seek first the Kingdom of God, ...and all these things shall be given to you."* (Matt 6:33). We had let go of each other, and God had given us back to each other and was now calling us both to a life of full time ministry. To put God first is to worship. To let go of anything or anyone that might stop you putting God first is sacrifice. When God calls us to let go we do so in obedience, and simply put our faith in God.

After worship and sacrifice, faith and obedience became prominent as the next two principles in the Bible's teaching on giving. The book of Hebrews says, *"By faith Abel offered a better sacrifice than Cain did. By faith he was commended as a righteous man, when God spoke well of his offerings."* (Heb 11:4). That faith included trusting God to provide for daily needs, which proved to be a big factor when the Israelites started to tithe.

There is a brief mention of tithing in Abraham's story (Gen 14:20), and then it is mentioned for the second time in the story of Abraham's grandson Jacob. He has just encountered God at Bethel, where he had gone to sleep and dreamed of a stairway reaching right up to heaven, with angels ascending and descending. On waking, Jacob is so overcome with the awareness of God's presence that he makes a vow, promising to give a tenth of everything to God, at the same time trusting that God would protect him and provide for his needs. *"Then Jacob made a vow saying, 'If God will be with me and will watch over me on this journey I am taking and will give me food to eat and clothes to wear so that I return safely to my father's house, then the Lord will be my God... and of all that you give me I will give you a tenth."* (Gen 28:20,21). This was before God commanded the Israelites to tithe, so in this case it was not a matter of obedience, but faith; faith that God would provide. In many cases that faith was tested by God, as we see in the story of manna from heaven.

Moving on from Genesis into Exodus, we find that the Israelites have been enslaved in Egypt for hundreds of years. The exodus itself is the story of how God delivered them from that bondage to slavery. God persuades Pharaoh to release the people through a series of ten plagues, culminating in the Angel of Death taking the life of every firstborn son and animal throughout Egypt. Prior to this, the Israelites are commanded to sacrifice a lamb and eat the roasted meat in their homes, with the blood of the lamb smeared on their doorposts. Having been told that the Angel of death would visit the land that night, they had to have faith that the blood of the lamb would save them. Moses had been told, *"When I see the blood, I will pass over you."* (Ex 12:13). Hence the annual celebration of the Passover Festival, culminating hundreds of years later in the death of Christ, the Lamb of God, on the Cross at Passover.

All the Israelites could do was to trust and obey. Sure enough, God's words came true, and despite every Egyptian household losing their firstborn son, every Israelite household covered by the blood of the lamb was kept safe. Not surprisingly, Pharaoh had had enough and urged the Israelites to leave as quickly as possible. The Egyptians even showered them with gifts of silver and gold in their urgency to get rid of these people who had brought them such trouble.

The Israelites came to the Red Sea and found it impossible to cross. By now Pharaoh had changed his mind about the wisdom of losing a million slaves, and was pursuing them with his army of soldiers and chariots. The people were trapped with the sea in front and Pharaoh's soldiers behind, and they cried out to Moses in despair and desperation. Again they were required to exercise faith and obedience.

"Then the Lord said to Moses, 'Why are you crying out to me? Tell the Israelites to move on. Raise your staff and stretch out your hand over the sea to divide the water so that the Israelites can go through the sea on dry ground'... Then Moses stretched out his hand over the sea, and all that night the Lord drove the sea back with a strong east wind and turned it into dry land. The waters were divided, and the Israelites went through the sea on dry ground, with a wall of water on their right and on their left." (Ex 14:15,16; 21,22).

The Israelites came through the Red Sea safe and dry, but Pharaoh's pursuing chariots were drowned as the waters came rushing back in a flood. The people were safe but they still needed to trust God, and they didn't find it easy. They entered the Wilderness, a great expanse of desert, and they soon became hungry and thirsty. In no time at all they forgot God's miraculous intervention and came to Moses grumbling and complaining about the lack of food and water. *"Then the Lord said to Moses, 'I will rain down bread from heaven for you. The people are to go out each day and gather enough for that day. In this way I will test them and see whether they will follow my instructions."* (Ex 16:4).

Sure enough, the next morning there was dew on the ground that looked like flakes of frost. The people gathered it up and ate it like bread. It was white like coriander seed and tasted like wafers of honey. They called the bread 'manna', which literally means, 'What is it?' On the first day they gathered what they had been told, and Moses told them not to save any for the next day, as God would provide fresh manna every morning. Some of them found it difficult to believe that God would keep providing fresh manna so they kept some manna in reserve 'just in case'. *"..they kept part of (the manna) until morning, but it was full of maggots and began to smell. So Moses was angry with them."* (Ex 16:20).

Again God tested them by commanding them not to gather manna on the Sabbath, which was a day of rest, but to gather twice as much as usual on the sixth day, and keep enough overnight for the Sabbath. Now they needed faith to believe that on the sixth day the extra manna would not rot, even though it rotted every other time that some was kept overnight. *"Nevertheless, some of the people went out on the seventh day to gather it, but found none. Then the Lord said to Moses, 'How long will you refuse to keep my commands and my instructions?"* (Ex 16:27, 28).

Time after time the people struggled to trust God and obey him. And yet throughout that time in the wilderness, God faithfully provided. The Bible records that this manna appeared on the ground every day of the forty years they wandered in the desert. In Joshua we read that they eventually crossed over the Jordan into Canaan, and when they camped at Gilgal four days later, they celebrated the Passover for the first time in the Promised Land. *"The day after the Passover, that very day, they ate some of the produce of the land; unleavened bread and roasted grain. The manna stopped the day after they ate this food from the land; there was no longer any manna for the Israelites, but that year they ate of the produce of Canaan."* (Josh 5:11,12).

It was not only bread that God provided in the desert. When the Israelites first grumbled about the lack of food, God sent a flock of quail which fell on the camp, and when they complained about the lack of water, God told Moses to "*Strike the rock, and water will come out of it for the people to drink.*" (Ex 17:6). Moses did so and water poured out of the rock. Moses called that place, Massah, which means 'testing'. The people were complaining and 'testing' God, not really believing that God would provide for their needs. At the same time, God tested the people to see if they would have faith in his provision and be obedient to his commands. "*In this way I will test them and see whether they will follow my instructions.*" (Ex 16:4)

There are some huge lessons here in the context of giving. We saw from the beginning how God loves to give and to bless his people. The problem is that even his own people don't believe that God is so good. They doubt him and have no faith in his provision. One of the reasons that many of us today don't give to the poor as much as we might is that we are concerned about our own needs, not having the faith that if we will provide for others, so God will provide for us. God does not provide at random, regardless of peoples' faith or lack of faith. If we have faith in God, and express that faith through obedience to his commands, then God will provide.

As the people settled down in the land God had given them, he gave them clear instructions on how they should live under his rule. He gave the Ten Commandments on Mount Sinai, and then a whole list of rules as to how they should live and worship. The book of Leviticus contains specific regulations as to how they were to offer particular offerings and sacrifices, with stern warnings as to what would happen if they disobeyed. The whole of Deuteronomy 28 is concerned with the blessings that would follow obedience, and the curses that would result from disobedience.

This strict emphasis on the Law and stern warning about disobedience can sound very harsh and legalistic to Christians whose faith is founded on the love of God and the grace of Christ. But think of it this way. Most parents want their children to grow up as loving, caring and sharing individuals, but new parents can be quite shocked at the unwillingness of their two year old to share his toys. Most children of that age don't share naturally; they have to be taught. Sometimes that teaching has to start with them being told to share, whether they want to or not. As they get older and (hopefully) pick up their parents' example of giving and sharing, they will learn to give willingly from the heart, but most children first have to learn to do as they are told. This is what we see happening in God's dealings with his children in the Old Testament.

The blessing of God in response to faith and obedience is clearly seen in the example of King Solomon, on the occasion of him coming to the throne as a young man. During the reign of his father David, the kingdom of Israel had grown into a huge empire, and the prospect of ruling over that great empire was no doubt a daunting one for young Solomon. The story begins with an example of how ready and willing God is to give and to bless, and a reminder that sometimes we need to have the faith to ask.

"At Gibeon the Lord appeared to Solomon during the night in a dream and God said, 'Ask for whatever you want me to give you." (1 Kings 3:5). The young king humbly acknowledges his inexperience and lack of ability for the task ahead of him, and asks God for wisdom and discernment.

"The Lord was pleased that Solomon had asked for this. So God said to him, 'Since you have asked for this and not for long life or wealth for yourself, nor have asked for the death of your enemies but for discernment in administering justice, I will do what you have asked. I will give you a wise and discerning heart, so that there will never have been anyone like you, nor will there ever be. Moreover, I

will give you what you have not asked for – both riches and honour – so that in your lifetime you will have no equal among kings. And if you walk in my statutes and commands as David your father did, I will give you a long life." (1 Kings 3:10-14).

As always, God was true to his word and kings and queens from neighbouring nations came to marvel at Solomon's wisdom and riches.

At this point in my biblical journey I had learned the key principles of worship, sacrifice, faith, obedience and blessing. All five principles came together in Genesis 22. The story of Abraham and Isaac and an incredible act of giving.

6 The Mountain of The Lord

In 1992 Penny and I had an opportunity to visit the Holy Land. On the first morning our Israeli guide took us across the Kidron Valley from where we enjoyed a panoramic view of Jerusalem. In the centre of the Holy City is the Dome of the Rock, venerated by Muslims the world over. Muslims have huge respect for Abraham, whom they see as the Father of the Faith. Legend has it that this beautiful golden dome is built on the very spot on Mount Moriah where Abraham prepared to offer up his son Isaac as a sacrifice to God. I had never realised before that Mount Moriah is part and parcel of Mount Zion, where King David built his own city, later to be known as Jerusalem. The Temple itself is built on the spot where David had earlier built an altar on the threshing floor of Araunah (2 Chron 3:1). On that same mountain hundreds of years later, Jesus of Nazareth was taken to the hill called Calvary to be crucified, paying the ultimate sacrifice for the sins of all mankind. The place where Abraham was called to sacrifice his son Isaac, where David refused to make a sacrifice that cost him nothing, is the same mountain where God himself gave up his son to be crucified: the Mountain of the Lord.

Just a few years earlier when I was studying for the ministry, one of our lecturers had drawn a simple black cross in the centre of a large whiteboard. Standing back and looking at the cross he said, "That... is the centre of world history." He justified his comment by reminding us how historians have dated world history before and after Christ – BC and AD. I was reminded of his comment when I stood looking at the Mountain of the Lord, the place where it all came together. Some years earlier the story of Abraham and Isaac had played a significant part in my call to the ministry. Now, as I reflected on the significance of this Mountain of the Lord, and the story of Abraham being asked to sacrifice his son, everything came together.

The Mountain of the Lord, the place where God provides, is first and foremost a place of worship. In order for that worship to occur, it had also to be a place of sacrifice. The sacrifice only took place because God commanded it, which is why the Mountain of the Lord is also a place of obedience. This was obedience to a God who commanded Abraham to sacrifice his son, despite the fact that the promises of God could only be realised if his son had children. This obedience therefore required faith. Faith that God could be trusted, no matter what the circumstances. And when Abraham obeyed in faith, and showed he was prepared to make a sacrifice of worship, God responded with blessing, not only providing a ram for the sacrifice, but promising that Abraham's descendants would be blessed, and become as numerous as the stars in the sky and the sand on the seashore.

The Mountain of the Lord, the place where God promises to provide, is the place of worship, the place of sacrifice, the place of obedience, the place of faith, and the place of blessing. In this one story we see God opening up the fingers of mankind's clenched fist, one by one, teaching us to give as God gives. The five fingers represent the five principles that are central to the Old Testament teaching on giving.

SACRIFICE

"Some time later God tested Abraham. He said to him, 'Abraham!' 'Here I am.' he replied. Then God said, 'Take your son, your only son, Isaac, whom you love, and go to the region of Moriah. Sacrifice him there as a burnt offering on one of the mountains I will tell you about." (Gen 22:1,2).

In terms of sacrifice or letting go, you can't get more challenging than this. Abraham had been promised by God that his descendants would become a great nation (Gen 12:2). He married a beautiful woman called Sarah but for many years they were childless. Then in Gen 18:10 the Lord appears to Abraham and says that by the following year his wife Sarah will bear him a son. Abraham was already 99 years old and Sarah much the same age. Not surprisingly Sarah laughed in disbelief when she heard the news, but God kept his promise, and nine months later their one and only son was born. They named him Isaac which means "laughter", and he became a joy and delight to them, and the apple of Abraham's eye. Imagine then how Abraham must have felt when God told him to sacrifice his son.

For Abraham, the mountain of the Lord that day was both a literal sacrifice with a life to be offered on the altar, and a personal sacrifice which would cost Abraham dear. Sacrifice is the Old Testament equivalent of 'letting go'. To sacrifice is to take something (or someone) precious to you and hand it over. To give it up. To let go, even unto death. It's where God brings us face to face with our human tendency to take and keep, and says, "Come on. Give it to me."

Sacrifice costs. Without cost there is no sacrifice. We've seen this with David at the threshing floor, and when Abel brought the biggest and best as an offering. The cost of the sacrifice may be financial; it may be emotional; it may be physical or psychological. But if it doesn't really cost us anything, then it can hardly be said to be a sacrifice.

OBEDIENCE

"Early the next morning Abraham got up and saddled his donkey. He took with him two of his servants and his son Isaac. When he had cut enough wood for the burnt offering, he set out for the place God had told him about." (Gen 22:3).

It says in verse one that God tested Abraham. Another test of faith and obedience. But this was huge. Would Abraham be obedient to God and let go of his precious son, or would he refuse? Abraham passed the test. The Bible tells us that he never questioned God, he never protested, nor did he try to put off the evil day. Amazingly, he passed the test of obedience with flying colours. Not only did he obey immediately, setting off early the next morning, but not one word of protest or bargaining passed his lips. Moreover, when the final moment came and Isaac was bound on the altar, verse 10 tells us that Abraham *"reached out his hand and took the knife to slay his son"*. It would appear that Abraham had every intention of following through his obedience to the Lord's command.

Some will ask, "Why does God do this? Is he a sadist?" The answer is clearly no. The ultimate sacrifice was made by Jesus on the cross. Let's be clear that this was also the ultimate act of obedience. Being beaten, flogged and crucified was the last thing that Jesus would have chosen to endure, if it could have been avoided. In such anguish that his sweat fell like drops of blood to the ground, Jesus prayed, *"Father, if you are willing, take this cup from me; yet not my will, but yours be done."* (Lk 22:42). Paul describes Jesus as humbling himself and becoming obedient to death - even death on a cross. (Php 2:8). Jesus made this ultimate act of sacrifice and obedience on our behalf, but we are still called to make the sacrifice of denying self, and to pledge obedience to our Lord who calls us to follow him. Denying self can sound very negative, but when our self is by nature sinful, the act of denying self actually sets us free to be as God intended us, experiencing true freedom and fulfilment.

Apart from rare occasions like that of Abel, without obedience the sacrifice will not happen. Remember our context. The Lord is faced with a people who have become selfish and unwilling to let go and give. One way to teach them to give is to emphasise the discipline of sacrifice. Because sacrifice is always going to be hard, the Lord removes any choice and makes it a command to be obeyed. Thus the essence of worship in the Old Testament was the command to sacrifice. The form, details, and time of annual and occasional sacrifices became central to the Law.

With the New Testament emphasis on grace not law, Christians can sometimes forget the absolute importance of obeying God. Obedience to Christ is foundational to being a disciple. Jesus said, *"If you love me, you will obey what I command."* (Jn 14:15). In Jesus' story of the man building his house on rock, we often assume that the rock is Jesus, and as long as we have faith in Christ, then our lives are built on the rock. A closer examination reveals a different emphasis. Jesus said, *"Everyone who hears these words of mine <u>and puts them into practice</u> is like a wise man who built his house on the rock."* (Matt 7:24) Whatever we discover in our search for the Bible's teaching on giving, we need to put into practice. If we hear, but do not obey, we will be building our house on sand.

WORSHIP

"On the third day Abraham looked up and saw the place in the distance. He said to his servants, 'Stay here with the donkey while I and the boy go over there. We will worship and then we will come back to you." (Gen 22:4,5).

Notice the word that Abraham uses. We will worship. He is about to give up his son to God. About to let go of that which is more precious to him than anyone or anything else in the whole world. Remember that God's promise of a nation coming from Abraham rests on this boy Isaac. And how does Abraham describe this incredibly painful letting go? Worship.

As God teaches us to let go and give, the first finger of the closed fist that needs to open, is called worship. What Abraham did on Mount Moriah is all in the context of worship. The Lord was his God and he honoured God above all else, even his son. As he told his servants to wait while he took his son to the mountain, he was preparing to worship, with obedience and sacrifice. We learn to give when we focus first on God and realise who he is and what he has done for us in Christ. Cain and Abel worshipped God by making an offering. No-one told them to, it was simply man's natural response to who God is. And how did they worship? They gave. From that point on, the word 'offering' was synonymous with worship. Whether it is an offering of praise and adoration, of confession and intercession, of our finances or our bodies and all that we are, we offer ourselves, we give ourselves to God in worship. To give is to worship. To worship is to give. When God commanded the Israelites to worship, he was teaching them to give.

Christians today need to recognise that our financial giving is first and foremost an act of worship. Paul instructed the early church to set aside their offering for the poor *'on the first day of every week'* (1 Cor 16:2). It was part of their Sunday worship. When he praises the Macedonian church for their generous giving to the poor, he says that *'they gave themselves first to the Lord and then to us in keeping with God's will.'* (2 Cor 8:5). Our offering of money is very much a part of our worship. When I agonised at Spring Harvest over how much we should give, the over-riding factor was the context of worship. The literal meaning of the word worship has to do with 'worth' – giving God his worth. How could I honour God as my Lord and then not give him his worth in my offering?

FAITH

"Abraham took the wood for the burnt offering and placed it on his son Isaac, and he himself carried the fire and the knife. As the two of them went on together, Isaac spoke up and said to his father Abraham, 'Father?' 'Yes my son,' Abraham replied. 'The fire and the wood are here,' Isaac said, 'but where is the lamb for the burnt offering?' Abraham answered, 'God himself will provide the lamb for the burnt offering, my son.' And the two of them went on together." (Gen 22:6-8).

They leave the servants behind, and together the old man and the young boy begin to climb. Picture the scene. An old man and his young son, making their way together up the steep mountain. Abraham's heart was heavy with sorrow, but Isaac's heart was light with innocence, full of trust and curiosity. You can almost hear the young boy say, 'Dad? Dad, where's the lamb for the burnt offering Dad?' We can only imagine what was going through Abraham's heart and mind as he answers, '*God himself will provide the lamb for the burnt offering, my son.*'

What an incredibly prophetic picture. Hundreds of years later, Father God brought his only begotten son to that same place, and through his son provided the lamb. The Lamb of God, who takes away the sin of the world. The writer to the Hebrews remembers Abraham not for his sacrifice and obedience, but for his faith. In fact Abraham becomes known as the father of the faithful.

Why is faith or trust so important in our context? The answer is that when we feel prompted to give to the needs of others, our first concern is, "What about our needs? Who will look after us, while we're busy looking after others?" The question is equally applicable to someone faced with giving up a loved one, as it is to someone being asked to give a substantial amount of their income or capital. If our security is closely connected to the person or possessions we are being commanded to give up, then where will we look for our security? The answer is God, through the avenue of faith. Sometimes, as with Abraham on Mount Moriah, the sacrifice is so great that all you can do is trust God.

As we learn to trust God, and God proves himself more than trustworthy, sometimes in miraculous ways, so our faith grows and we are more able to give whatever is asked without worrying about the outcome. So our ability to give cheerfully and willingly grows.

Anecdotal evidence would suggest that when God provides, he does seem to make a point of leaving things until the last minute, as he did with Abraham. Our minister in Ludlow, Colin Waltham, had previously been a missionary in Indonesia. On one occasion he and his wife had to leave the country at short notice and return home. They had no money for the air fare, and the only way they could raise the money was to sell their car. They booked the tickets and then advertised the car for sale, but had no takers. The airport was many hours journey away, and the day before they were due to fly, they still had not been able to sell the car. Believing that God wanted them on that flight, they decided to undertake the long journey and trust that somehow they would be provided with money for the tickets. They arrived at the airport with only an hour to spare before take-off. Within one hour they had sold the car, bought the tickets, and were flying home! They realised afterwards that if they had sold the car earlier, they would have had no transport to get them to the airport. God knows all our needs and he can be trusted. When God appears to leave things until the last minute, it may well stretch our faith, but the end result is that our faith is strengthened. The next time we are in a similar situation, the memory of the previous "last minute" provision will encourage us to trust God all the more. Like an athlete exercising her muscles, every experience of trusting in God's provision builds our faith.

There is one significant difference in the sacrifice that God made when he gave up his Son to be crucified, and the sacrifice that was asked of Abraham on Mount Moriah. The difference is that when Abraham trusted God and gave up his son to the Lord in obedience, at the very last moment God stepped in. *"Do not lay a hand on the boy,' he said, 'Do not do anything to him. Now I know that you fear God, because you have not withheld from me your son, your only son."* (Gen 22:12). Abraham looked up and there was a ram caught in the thicket. He had been prepared to let go of his precious son, but God provided a substitute, and Abraham sacrificed the ram as a burnt offering in worship to God. The time of testing can be extremely hard, especially when it involves something or someone very precious to you, but the point is that God provided. The verse that follows is to me the key verse of the whole chapter. *"So Abraham called that place The Lord Will Provide. And to this day it is said, 'On the mountain of the Lord it will be provided."* (Gen 22:14).

You may be familiar with one of the Hebrew names for God, 'Jehovah Jireh', meaning The Lord Will Provide. But did you realise that it comes from this very passage, and is in fact the name of a mountain? The name gave rise to a Hebrew saying, 'On the mountain of the Lord it will be provided."

BLESSING

"The angel of the Lord called to Abraham from heaven a second time and said, 'I swear by myself, declares the Lord, that because you have done this and have not withheld your son, your only son, I will surely bless you and make your descendants as numerous as the stars in the sky and as the sand on the seashore. Your descendants will take possession of the cities of their enemies, and through your offspring all nations on earth will be blessed, because you have obeyed me." (Gen 22:15-18).

The fifth finger, or thumb, is opened by blessing. The thumb is appropriate because worship, sacrifice, obedience and faith all flow from us towards God. As the thumb touches each of the fingers, so blessing is God's response to each of the above. The blessing of God's provision that results from our obedience should be seen, not as a motive for giving, but as a tremendous boost to our faith. More often than not, the blessing overflows to others, as with the case of Abraham's descendants.

What is particularly significant here is the sheer far-reaching extent of the blessing that can come from one act of faith and obedience. Perhaps it's because in this one act of Abraham, we see such a huge expression of absolute trust in God. As I stood there in Jerusalem on that hot and dusty day in 1992, I reflected on the fact that the whole nation of Israel, with its tumultuous history from modern times, stretching right back to the Old Testament, came about as a result of one incredible act of worship, sacrifice, obedience and faith. It took place here, on the Mountain of the Lord, this centre of history where so many events have been overlaid, one on top of the other, culminating in the giving of God, when he loved the world so much he gave his Son.

7 God Teaches Tithing

"The purpose of tithing is to teach you always to put God first in your lives." (Dt 14:23 TLB)

If letting go can hurt, then for many people, tithing is a hurt too far! However, as I continued my biblical journey looking for God's teaching on giving, it soon became obvious that the principles of worship, sacrifice, obedience, faith and blessing, all came to be enshrined in the principles and practice of tithing. If God the Father was teaching his child to open the closed fist and learn to give and share, tithing seemed to be a crash course in opening all five fingers at once. That open hand must then learn to give willingly, cheerfully and generously, which is the emphasis of the New Testament.

Tithing is referred to throughout the Old Testament from Genesis to Malachi, but for our purpose here it would help to focus on just one passage, and to go through it in detail. The passage we're going to look at is Deuteronomy 14:22-29.

"Be sure to set aside a tenth of all that your fields produce each year. Eat the tithe of your grain, new wine and oil, and the firstborn of your herds and flocks in the presence of the Lord your God at the place he will choose as a dwelling for his Name, so that you may learn to revere the Lord your God always. But if that place is too distant and you have been blessed by the Lord your God and cannot carry your tithe (because the place where the Lord will choose to put his name is too far away), then exchange your

tithe for silver, and take the silver with you and go to the place the Lord your God will choose. Use the silver to buy whatever you like; cattle, sheep, wine or other fermented drink, or anything you wish. Then you and your household will eat there in the presence of the Lord your God and rejoice. And do not neglect the Levites living in your towns, for they have no allotment or inheritance of their own. At the end of every three years, bring all the tithes of that year's produce and store it in your towns, so that the Levites (who have no allotment or inheritance of their own) and the aliens, the fatherless and the widows who live in your towns may come and eat and be satisfied, and so that the Lord your God may bless you in all the work of your hands."

TITHING AS SACRIFICE AND OBEDIENCE

"Be sure to set aside a tenth…"

For most people the very mention of ten per cent is enough to put them off tithing. Ten per cent seems just too much. How can anyone reasonably be asked to give ten per cent of their income to God/ the church/ the poor? How on earth can we be expected to survive on only 90% of our income when we have all these bills to pay? But that's the whole point. Tithing as a system of giving ensures that whether we are rich or poor, our giving will always be a sacrifice. The poor feel they can't possibly live on what's left, and the rich struggle to give so much away. No-one's happy, because it's a real sacrifice for everyone. At the end of the day, sacrifice is sacrifice, and if there's no inherent sacrifice in our giving then our giving is not honouring to God, as David makes clear in 2 Samuel 24.

Because sacrifice on this scale is so far removed from our human nature and 'tightfistedness', the Lord saw fit to make it a command. Although Abraham and Jacob gave a tenth in response to God's blessing and provision, God could not rely on the Israelites always being so responsive and so he made tithing a command, ensuring that obedience became an essential part of their giving.

For me personally, the fact that tithing is always a sacrifice makes my tithe a meaningful part of my worship. By contrast, putting a handful of coins into the collection plate can hardly count as either worship or obedience. Again, through the act of tithing I know I am being obedient, and practising obedience on a regular basis is key to being a disciple.

TITHING AS WORSHIP

"Eat the tithe of your grain, new wine and oil, and the firstborn of your herds and flocks in the presence of the Lord your God at the place he will choose as a dwelling for his Name."

In the days when worship involved feasting, tithing became an essential part of communal worship. In fact, without the tithe, such worship would have been impossible on any community or national scale. However, the earliest examples of tithing involve individuals spontaneously worshipping God, long before tithing became enshrined in the law.

The first mention of tithing is in relation to Abraham, the 'Father of the Faith'. In Genesis 14, Abraham's nephew Lot, together with his family and possessions, are kidnapped and carried off during a feud between warring kings. When Abraham hears what has happened, he calls out his own army of 300 men and goes in pursuit. He successfully recovers Lot and his family and possessions, and on his return home he is met by the mysterious priest/king Melchizedek, who many theologians see as symbolically representing Christ. In Gen 14:18-20 we read,

"Then Melchizedek king of Salem brought out bread and wine. He was priest of God Most High, and he blessed Abram, saying, 'Blessed be Abram by God Most High, Creator of heaven and earth. And blessed be God Most High, who delivered your enemies into your hand. Then Abram gave him a tenth of everything."

The second mention of tithing is the incident with Jacob at Bethel, which we saw in a previous chapter. Both Abraham and

Jacob tithed long before tithing became a part of the law given through Moses hundreds of years later. They gave their tithe to God in response to his blessing and provision. They gave their tithe in worship.

Even when tithing becomes part of the Law, given to Moses on Mount Sinai, it was still in the context of worship, giving God his worth. The Jews were adamant that the tithe belonged to God. If they were to worship (giving God his worth) they at least had to start by giving to God what belonged to him in the first place. Leviticus 27:30 is clear. "A *tithe of everything from the land, whether grain from the soil or fruit from the trees, belongs to the Lord; it is holy to the Lord.*" This assertion is again clearly implied in Malachi 3:8,9 where the Israelites are accused of robbing God because they have not brought the whole tithe into the storehouse. Giving God what belongs to him is a key principle in the practice of tithing.

Secondly, in the context of worship, tithing teaches us to give God the best (*the firstborn of your herds and flocks*). In tithing we give not only ten per cent, but the FIRST ten per cent. In other words we give that ten per cent to God straight away, rather than paying the bills first and then seeing if we can afford the tithe. Ten per cent may seem a lot when you're not used to it, but in practice we are following the example of Abel by giving today's equivalent of the biggest and best. It really is a matter of attitude.

When the church at Broad Haven first agreed to tithe the church income, it shouldn't really have been a big deal, because the accounts showed that we were already giving roughly ten per cent of our income to mission and other work outside the local church. But it was a big deal, for the following reason. Previously, the church had paid their bills first, then looked to see what was left over and therefore what they could afford to give away. In agreeing to tithe, we agreed on a fundamental shift of attitude. From now on, whatever came in, and despite whatever bills we might have to pay, we were committing ourselves to give the FIRST ten per cent to God. It was a small but fundamental difference, which began to bring us in line with the teaching of Jesus. That is, to seek FIRST his Kingdom, and trust that God will provide for our needs.

I cannot emphasise enough that this is a key factor in tithing. In giving God the first ten per cent we are learning to put God first, and to trust him to provide. In putting God first before all things we come to the very centre of what worship is all about.

TITHING TEACHES US TO REVERE THE LORD OUR GOD, WHICH BUILDS OUR FAITH

"Be sure to set aside a tenth… so that you may learn to revere the Lord your God always."

One of the greatest blessings I have found in tithing is that the actual practice of tithing has helped me to grow in my relationship with God, helping me to grow in faith and to revere the Lord my God. Deuteronomy states that the Israelites would experience the same thing as they obeyed the command to tithe.

How does this happen in practice? We need to remember that the discipline of giving ten per cent of all their crops and livestock was just as big a sacrifice then, as giving ten per cent of our income is today. But as the Israelites responded in obedience, so the Lord responded in blessing. Practical blessings that could be seen and measured, and which led to the Israelites learning to revere their God. God's promise to bless their obedience is spelt out in detail in Deuteronomy 28:2-6.

"All these blessings will come upon you and accompany you if you obey the Lord your God – You will be blessed in the city and blessed in the country. The fruit of your womb will be blessed, and the crops of your land and the young of your livestock – the calves of your herds and the lambs of your flocks. Your basket and your kneading

trough will be blessed. You will be blessed when you come in and blessed when you come out."

Penny and I began tithing when we went to college to train for the ministry and almost straightaway some unusual things began to happen. Giving up my job and moving to Cardiff with three young children was a real strain on our finances, but it soon became evident that we were being looked after. Not long after we arrived in Cardiff we were faced with a bill for £98, and not enough money in the bank to pay it. In the same post we received a gift for £100, from friends whom we hadn't seen for years. They had heard we were training for the ministry and wanted to bless us.

We have had many such experiences then and since. In 2005 I was planning to go on a three month sabbatical, and Penny and I were hoping to include a trip to the Airport Vineyard Church in Toronto. Even with cheap flights from Cardiff, we still needed £1,000 for the two of us to make the trip and have accommodation for the week. At the time we just didn't have the money but we really felt God wanted us to go so we prayed that the money would be provided.

That same week I had been asked to lead a day retreat for a local Churches Together group. They were meeting all day Saturday in the Village Hall opposite our house. I spoke in the morning, and announced that after lunch I would be teaching on Giving, and how God provides when we put him first. While everyone else was having their sandwiches Penny and I went across the road to the house for lunch. I was aware that most of my examples of God's provision were a bit out of date, so I asked God to give me a more up to date illustration. In our village the post tends to arrive late, and in fact it arrived while we were eating lunch. Amongst the post was a letter from my Dad saying that an elderly Aunt had died in New Zealand. She had no immediate family, and had left a legacy to be shared out amongst the family. My share of the legacy was enclosed in the envelope. A cheque for £1,000! Exactly what we needed to go to Toronto.

I went back after lunch, gave the talk, and said, "Now let me give you an up to date illustration. While we were having lunch half an hour ago…" Of course these things don't happen all the time, but it does introduce a "wow" factor and consequently teaches us to revere the Lord our God.

When I stop and look back over the last thirty years, I think I can honestly say the one thing more than anything else that has caused us to grow in our faith and in our reverence and deep respect for God, is the actual practice of tithing and the things that have happened as a result. As it says in the Living Bible translation, *"The purpose of tithing is to teach you always to put God first in your lives."* (Dt 14:23 TLB).

TITHING AS A PRINCIPLE, NOT A PRESCRIPTION

"But if that place is too distant and you have been blessed by the Lord your God and cannot carry your tithe (because the place where the Lord will choose to put his name is too far away), then exchange your tithe for silver, and take the silver with you and go to the place the Lord your God will choose. Use the silver to buy whatever you like; cattle, sheep, wine or other fermented drink, or anything you wish. Then you and your household will eat there in the presence of the Lord your God and rejoice."

What I love about this next part of the passage is its flexibility. After emphasising the need to select the firstborn, usually the biggest and best, it then goes on to say that if you have too far to travel… don't worry about it. Sell your animals and crops and bring the equivalent in money. If the Lord chooses to be worshipped somewhere else, then go there. When you're ready to worship God with a feast, buy whatever you like… anything you wish. It's reminiscent of a BBQ where everyone brings their own meat, or a bottle party where people bring their own favourite tipple. (I don't want to offend those who are teetotal, but the passage does include wine, and the fermented drink means beer).

The key sentence is at the end of verse 26. *"Then you and your household will eat there in the presence of the Lord your God and REJOICE."* This might seem strange for those who are used to seeing tithing as a legalistic Old Testament command, but its whole purpose was to enable the people of God to come together in God's presence and have a party. Not a secular party, but real worship, full of joy, enjoying fellowship with God and with each other. Does that sound like tithing? If it doesn't then it should.

One of the problems with the practice of tithing today is that many people, preachers and others, make it too legalistic. What started as a straight forward command becomes laden with questions. Do we tithe before tax or after tax? Do we include gifts, grants, or just regular income? Surely tithing was just for farmers? If we don't have animals or crops, does tithing have anything to do with us? Do we give the whole tithe to the church, or can we give it where we see fit? What about those who don't tithe? Is it a matter of individual choice, or are we duty bound to tell everyone who doesn't tithe that they are robbing God?

These and many other questions seem to me to display a legalistic frame of mind that can equally beset both those who are pro-tithing, and those who are anti-tithing. I am reminded of Jesus' parable about the self-righteous Pharisee in Luke 18. He boasted before God that he fasted twice a week and tithed everything he had. God was not impressed. Where tithing is concerned it's far more important to get our attitude right than getting details right.

The principle of tithing is simple and clear. Everything belongs to God, including what we are given, and what we earn through hard work. It all belongs to God and comes from God. So let's acknowledge God's place in our lives by giving back to him at least the first ten per cent. In doing so we acknowledge him as our creator and Lord, and we also acknowledge that we will trust him to provide for our own needs through the remaining 90%. In giving the first ten per cent we also bless God with our worship, bless the ongoing ministry of the church, and bless those who are in need.

Having reflected on the principle and practice of tithing for some time, it seems to me that tithing is God's way of giving the Christian church a beginner's course on giving. Not a legalistic "how to" course, but an exciting introduction to giving in the light of God's outrageous extravagance. In that context, tithing teaches us to walk before we run.

TITHING AS A MEANS OF SUPPORTING MINISTRY

"And do not neglect the Levites living in your towns, for they have no allotment or inheritance of their own."

One of the results of the Israelites' obedience to the tithe was that it provided for ministry in terms of supporting the Levites. When the twelve tribes settled in the land of Canaan they were all given a particular piece of land as an inheritance. The tribe of Levi however received no such inheritance. They were to have a special role in serving in the Temple, and all the priests came from their tribe. Deuteronomy 14:27,28 makes it clear that this priestly tribe were to be provided for through the tithe. If ever the Israelites neglected to tithe then the ministry suffered, as is made abundantly clear in Nehemiah 13:10,11. *"I also learned that the portions assigned to the Levites had not been given to them, and that all the Levites and singers responsible for the service had gone back to their own fields. So I rebuked the officials and asked them, "Why is the house of God neglected? Then I called them together and stationed them at their posts."*

In many churches and chapels today there is a lack of spiritual food because the tithe has been neglected and the church cannot afford regular full time trained ministry from men and women called by God. Some people say the reason is the lack of people being called to the ministry, but this is not true. In Wales there have been many young men and women called and trained who were eager to minister in Wales. Unfortunately many could not find a position which did not include ministering to a large group of churches. Despondent and frustrated, they accepted a call to churches in other parts of the country that were prepared to pay them to minister to one church.

Why is the house of God neglected? That's a question that could be asked again and again. Ministering as I do in Wales, I am aware that churches and chapels are closing at the rate of one a week. Some denominations try to ensure that each church is covered to some extent by ordained clergy. One result of this policy is that some ministers find themselves struggling to minister to as many as 20 different churches. In the Baptist denomination each chapel is responsible for maintaining their own minister, either solely or as part of a group. In this context there are large tracts of Wales where there are many chapels but not one full time minister for miles. When I came to Breconshire, the Baptist Union of Wales had 19 chapels in the County without one minister between them. Many such chapels have banded together in groups of four, five, six or more in order to support a minister. Such efforts usually do little more than delay the end. One minister rushing around trying to keep things going is not an effective way to advance the kingdom or build the church.

The Challenge to Change Survey in 1995 [4] showed clearly that the only churches that were growing were those which had one church per minister. Many bemoaned the situation and asked how many chapels could possibly support their own minister. Yet it is a mathematical fact that it only takes ten people tithing to support a minister on a stipend equal to their average earnings. If more people tithed there could be many more churches and chapels in this country with their own minister. That in itself is

4   *Challenge to Change* – The 1995 Welsh Churches Survey, published by British and Foreign Bible Society

no guarantee to church growth, but it would certainly be a help in that direction.

TITHING PROVIDES FOR THOSE IN NEED

"At the end of every three years, bring all the tithes of that years produce and store it in your towns, so that the Levites... and the aliens, the fatherless and the widows who live in your towns may come and eat and be satisfied"

Every year, particularly at Christmas, many Christians and churches are inundated with mail shots from charities appealing for financial support. So often churches would love to give more, but feel unable to because they struggle to meet their own responsibilities. This is where I began to discover one of the joys of tithing. Quite simply, when you start tithing, assuming you have some sort of regular income, you ALWAYS have money to give away. That's the beauty of the first tenth belonging to God. It's not a case of working out whether you can afford the tithe, any more than someone on PAYE trying to tell their employer that they can't really afford to pay tax this week. The tax belongs to the taxman, and it gets taken off your pay at source. We need to have the same attitude with tithing. If I receive £100, then £10 already belongs to God. It's no good me paying the bills first and then seeing if I've got £10 left over. That £10 belongs to God before I even think of paying bills. Let me illustrate with a story.

I remember one of our first experiences of tithing when we were at college training for the ministry. Money was short and we were on benefits. During the summer when we had no termly grant from the college, the Housing Benefit didn't arrive until the very end of the holidays. Every jar on the mantelpiece, every spare pocket in every old coat had been searched, until there literally wasn't a spare penny anywhere in the house. Finally the Housing Benefit arrived; the princely sum of £800. After the initial relief of being able to pay the bills and buy some long overdue bits and pieces, plus a few small luxuries for the family, we realised we had another luxury. We had money to give away – a tithe of £80. It didn't take us long to decide where it was going. We knew another young family just a few streets away, in similar financial straits. They protested when we gave them the money and said we couldn't possibly afford it; but we said it wasn't ours to keep. It was God's money, and he wanted us to give it to them.

The joy came in different ways. For one, we knew exactly what it felt like to be in their position, which meant we could easily imagine what it must be like to receive an unexpected cheque for £80. Knowing what that must feel like for them, made us feel amazing. To know that we had been able to help them so much was a privilege beyond words. It was a feel good factor, size XXL.

It is often said that some people are too poor to tithe. My response is that if you don't have much money then you can't afford not to tithe! And the beauty of it is that when you're tithing you always have money to give away. If you only have £10 per week, it means that every week you have £1 to give away. You may choose to give that to the church, or a friend or someone in need, but it's yours to give as God directs.

Some will say, what about the bills? Well quite simply, if you're struggling on a low income then you will struggle, but in my experience someone earning £100 who tithes, seems to get along a lot better on £90 with God's help, than a person earning £100 who is not tithing. It's a matter of putting God first and trusting him to provide. Jesus taught the same principle when he was discussing how easy it is to start worrying about the practical day to day things such as what we are going to eat, drink, or wear. His answer was this. *"Seek first his kingdom and his righteousness, and all these things will be added to you as well."* (Matt 6:33).

When we look at the New Testament we see that generous giving to the needy was one of the outstanding features of the early church. Acts 2:45 tells us that *"Selling their possessions and goods, they gave to anyone as he had need."* Has it ever occurred to you that most of these new Christians filled with the Holy Spirit were from a Jewish background, and familiar with the practice of tithing? If charismatic Christians today started from where the Jerusalem church started, perhaps we might begin to see a similar result. Experience of tithing plus the influence of the Holy Spirit can be a powerful combination.

TITHING AS BLESSING

"Be sure to set aside a tenth… so that the Lord your God may bless you in all the work of your hands."

The reference to our time in college might suggest to some that if you tithe, God will keep you going, but only by the skin of your teeth. There are times when this can appear to be the case. I remember seeing a wonderful poster of a kitten hanging on to a washing line rather precariously by one little paw. The caption read, "Faith isn't faith until it's all you've got left to hang on to!"

The blessing of tithing is multi-faceted. Sometimes the blessing occurs through our faith being strengthened; through the fact that in different ways we learn to revere the Lord our God; through ministry being provided for in the church; through those in need being provided for as the church uses the tithe to bless the poor; and through financial and other blessing being bestowed on those who tithe.

That 'other blessing' can take various forms. As the church at Broad Haven began to tithe, we saw people being saved and baptised, and a growth in faith and unity throughout the church. When the Lord promises to those who tithe *'so much blessing you will not have room enough for it'*, who is to say what form that blessing may take? After the church at Broad Haven had been tithing for a number of years, there was so much blessing that we literally did not have room for all the people on a Sunday morning, and we had to have two Sunday morning services, which became the norm for many years.

God used tithing in the Old Testament as a very effective way of teaching his people to give. A way of giving that was fair for everyone and enshrined the principles of worship, sacrifice, obedience, faith and blessing, as well as providing for ministry and for the poor. In the Old Testament he taught his people to open their clenched fist, and in the New Testament he taught them to give with an open hand and an open heart, through the teachings of Christ and the power of the Holy Spirit. A crucial question we all have to consider is this: is tithing part of the Old Testament law which no longer applies to the Christian life, or do we retain it as a foundation on which to build?

Before we consider that question, and as we prepare to move from the Old Testament to the New, let's remind ourselves that the Old Testament is not all Law and dutiful obedience. The Old Testament is in many ways a preparation for the New, and even in the depths of Mosaic Law we find glimpses of giving from the heart, paving the way for what we find in the New Testament. Consider the following story from the book of Exodus.

Exodus 35 and 36 records a heart- warming story of how the Israelites gave generously and willingly towards the building of the Tabernacle, not out of duty and obedience, but from the heart. A selection of verses will suffice to give a flavour of the story.

"This is what the Lord has commanded... Everyone who is willing is to bring to the Lord an offering of gold, silver, bronze...And everyone who was willing and whose heart moved him came and brought an offering to the Lord...All the Israelite men and women who were willing brought to the Lord freewill offerings for all the work the Lord... had commanded them to do...And all the people continued to bring freewill offerings morning after morning... so all the skilled craftsman... said to Moses, 'The people are bringing more than enough for doing the work... so the people were restrained from bringing more, because what they had already was more than enough to do all the work." (Ex 35:4,5,21,22,29; Ex 36:3-7)

The Lord commanded that his people should give willingly, as their hearts moved them. A foretaste of Paul's teaching, where it says that, *"Each man should give what he has decided in his heart to give, not reluctantly or under compulsion, for God loves a cheerful giver."* (2 Cor 9:7) As we move from the Old Testament to the New, we are entering a new stage, but following the same journey. We move from open hands to an open heart.

"I will give you a new heart and put a new spirit in you; I will remove from you your heart of stone and give you a heart of flesh." (Ez 36:26)

PART 3

JESUS TEACHES GIVING WITH AN OPEN HEART

8 Giving From The Heart

"**F**or *where your treasure is, there your heart will be also.*"
(Matt 6:21)

Against the background of the Old Testament, the teaching of Jesus was completely new. We read again and again in the Gospels that the people were amazed by his teaching, and not least by the authority with which he spoke. "*The people were all so amazed that they asked each other, 'What is this? A new teaching – and with authority!'" (Mk 1:27)*. It was not only his authority over sickness and evil spirits that shocked the crowds, but also the content of his teaching, which to the Jews was new to the point of being revolutionary.

When it comes to giving, Jesus did not focus on the amount, as in a tenth, but on the attitude of the heart. "*So when you give to the needy, do not announce it with trumpets, as the hypocrites do in the synagogues and on the streets, to be honoured by men. I tell you the truth, they have received their reward in full. But when you give to the needy, do not let your left hand know what your right hand is doing, so that your giving may be in secret. Then your Father, who sees what is done in secret, will reward you.*" (Matt 6:2-4).

In our journey through the Old Testament we've focussed on the hand that takes and keeps, and how God opened the fingers of worship, sacrifice, faith, obedience and blessing, one at a time, and particularly through the command to tithe. I came to the New Testament knowing that Jesus says very little about tithing, and I was keen to see how the teaching would develop. What I discovered was that Jesus is not so much interested in opening our hands, as in opening our hearts. Paul says that *"Each man should give what he has decided in his heart"* (2 Cor 9:7). It soon became clear to me that in the New Testament the amount we give and how we give is not written in the Law. It's decided in the heart. God gives us freedom to decide in our heart how much we should give. Which makes the heart, and whatever influences the heart, absolutely paramount where giving is concerned.

I learned a hard lesson about the heart when we moved to Brecon. At the end of March 2009 Penny and I went for a two day retreat to Ffald y Brenin, the Christian Retreat Centre made famous in Roy Godwin's book 'The Grace Outpouring' [5]. We had been in Broad Haven for 21 years, and were beginning to think we might stay there until we retired. We'd had such a clear call to Broad Haven all those years ago, and we had decided that we would stay there until God made it clear he was calling us elsewhere.

We had a good two days, and felt very positive about the coming year. Before we left we went for a walk and ended up on a hill where a large cross had been erected. As we drew near the cross I felt a strong prompting to literally take hold of the cross and lay everything down. Everything – ourselves, our marriage, our ministry, the lot. I told Penny what I felt, and we both went to the cross and let go of everything, giving it all back to God. I didn't know why I was being prompted to do that, but it felt the right thing to do. Then we packed up and went home.

That night at three o'clock in the morning God woke me up. I didn't hear a voice or anything dramatic; it was just that one moment I was fast asleep and the next moment I was wide awake, and all I could think about was Breconshire. Penny's family had

---

5   Roy Godwin and Dave Roberts, *'The Grace Outpouring'* David C. Cook 2012

lived in Breconshire for over 40 years so I was familiar with the area, but the thoughts racing through my mind concerned the spiritual state of the county. Through my connection with the Baptist Union of Wales I was keenly aware that from a spiritual point of view Breconshire, to use the phrase I coined at the time, was on the cutting edge of decline. The situation amongst the Baptist chapels was dire. There were twenty chapels in the county without a single minister between them. They averaged eight members, most of whom were very elderly, and as I discovered afterwards, nearly half of them met for Sunday worship only once a month. Some of them less than that. The situation was truly desperate.

As I thought about Breconshire, the words of Jesus from Matthew 10 and Luke 10 came to mind. This is where Jesus sends the disciples two by two to the villages and towns ahead of him, to heal the sick and proclaim the gospel. They were to look for people of peace, stay where they were welcomed, and basically make disciples. As I lay there in bed with these words and thoughts coursing through my mind, I had the very strong impression that the Lord was calling Penny and I to go to Breconshire and make disciples. I was so wide awake that I got up, got dressed, went downstairs and sat writing in my notebook what I felt God was saying.

A number of things became crystal clear in my mind. We were not to minister in one place but to go from town to village making disciples. When I asked God how a few disciples here and there in different places could become a church, I felt him saying very clearly, "You make disciples – I will build my church." Which was rather ironic as for the previous twenty years my emphasis had been the other way round. I had been trying to build the church, hoping that God would make disciples. I felt strongly that we were not being called to pastor an existing church or to plant a new church. Simply concentrate on making disciples who would make disciples, and let God build his church how he wanted. There was a lot more but that's the gist of what I felt God was saying.

Without going into all the details, after much prayer and discussion during the following weeks and months, God confirmed this to Penny, and we both agreed that God was calling us to Breconshire. We shared our thoughts with the Baptist Union of Wales and amazingly they agreed to fund us, giving us a clean sheet to develop the ministry as we felt led. [6]The funding situation was strengthened when the Baptist Union of Great Britain offered to share the costs. So far, so good.

As soon as we had the green light from the Baptist Union we started looking for somewhere to live. On a long list of possible houses was a three bedroomed house not far from Brecon town. It didn't look much on the estate agent's details, but it was on our list so we went to have a look. When we arrived we discovered it was actually a small farmhouse set on a hill overlooking the valley below, with stunning views. The farmer had retired and as often happens the farm was being split up, with the house being sold separately, together with an adjoining four acre field, to make it more attractive. There was a large sheep shed at the end of the yard, which no one seemed to want, and the estate agent suggested it might be pulled down, as some potential buyers thought it spoilt the view. The house was damp and in poor condition, and it had been on the market for two years.

If you think about the Garden of Eden, this is the point in the story where the old serpent sneaks in. Only this time it was Adam he was after, not Eve.

Twenty five years previously I had been a cowman in my late twenties nursing a lifelong dream of one day having my own farm. God had called me into the ministry and my farming career had come to an abrupt halt. Now, as I stood in the old farmyard on

---

6   See Baptist Union video on YouTube, *"There's a light in the valley"* for a glimpse into this ministry (9 mins)

a sunny day in August, looking down at the valley below, I felt as though God was saying that I had been faithful all those years ago, giving up farming for the ministry, and now he was going to reward me by allowing me to do both together.

I couldn't believe what was happening. It was as though a tidal wave of possibilities had come out of nowhere and swept me off my feet. The thoughts raced through my mind as we followed the estate agent around the property.

If no one wanted the sheep shed then it wouldn't cost much extra to buy; the rest of the farm was being rented out and there was the possibility of renting or buying some extra ground to go with the four acre field, perhaps as much as thirty acres; there were other buildings on the yard that were up for negotiation; if I restricted myself to keeping sheep it wouldn't take a lot of my time so it wouldn't impinge too much on the ministry; I wasn't going to be tied to pastoral responsibilities in a church, which made it more possible; taking sheep to market would help me fit in with the local community and enable us to make connections as we went from village to village…

My mind quickly filled with possibilities and my pulse was racing. Thankfully Penny loved the location, despite the house being damp and needing a lot doing to it. She wasn't so sure about the extra acres, but she too had fallen in love with the place.

That night I couldn't sleep. Only this time I wasn't thinking about going from village to village making disciples. All I could think about was the farm. In my mind it was already a farm, not a house. I lay awake for hours, working out which fields would be best to buy; then going through the farm year in my mind, from January to December imagining what needed doing every month and working out how I would do it: where would be best for lambing? How best to manage the grazing? Which fields would be suitable for making hay? How much equipment would I need? And so on.

It felt as though an old well which had been blocked up and covered over for years had suddenly been opened up and had become a spring welling up and overflowing. The dream of having my own farm, which had lain dormant all these years was now becoming a reality and I could hardly believe it was happening.

It wasn't long before I made an offer for the house, the shed, and about 30 acres of land. We couldn't afford a lot of money and it was a low offer, so I wasn't surprised when it was rejected. But no problem. No one else seemed interested, and I was convinced that this was where God wanted us to be. Over the following months I made more offers, each about the same amount, but asking for less acreage, and eventually making an offer for the house and field as advertised, but with a bid to rent more acres as well. The offer was still too low and again it was rejected.

During this time Penny was still sold on the house, despite the damp, but she was getting quite concerned about the amount of time and attention I was giving to the farming side. What about this call to make disciples? I assured her that it was all part of the same package, but we had to buy the place first and get that sorted before anything else could happen.

Then I got the phone call. Someone else had offered the asking price for the house. As I'd shown a lot of interest, I was being invited to better the offer before they accepted it. We hadn't yet sold our own house and we couldn't be sure what we would get for it, and I had to say no. I put the phone down in a state of shock. The bottom had dropped out of my world. I couldn't believe what had just happened. I felt numb.

We started looking for somewhere else to live, and found a lovely three bedroomed house with a small garden, next to open common land, and a stream running alongside. Penny was absolutely delighted. We made an offer, it was accepted, and we moved into our new home, ready to start this exciting ministry.

Except that if I'm honest, I found it hard to be excited. The bottom had dropped out of my world, and I was having trouble putting it back again. God started doing stuff, including a local farmer having an encounter with God that changed his life; people coming for prayer for healing; and a builder who met with God on the roof after his wife had been baptised. It was slow, but things were happening. At least on the surface. Underneath I felt empty. For the next few years, and I mean years, I would pass a small farm for sale and start dreaming again. I would look at some fields nearby and wonder how much they would cost to rent.

Eventually, after a lot of struggling, I did what I've always had to do, but this one took a long time. I let go. I finally let go of my dream; I let go of my desire to farm; I let go, and thankfully the Lord took it away. The battle for my heart was over. I was wounded and bruised, but I recovered.

God gives us free will. He wants us to love, give, and bless one another from the heart because we want to, not because we're being told. He wants us to want to give. Having been taught to open our clenched fist that used to take and keep, we now have the ability to give and share generously, but God won't make us. He wants us to give from the heart. They say you can take a horse to water, but you can't make it drink. As I read through the gospels with this new focus it became clear that Jesus was engaging in a battle for the heart.

The battle for the heart began in the Garden of Eden, with Adam and Eve being the first casualties, and continued in Genesis 4, with Cain and Abel. Cain was angry when his offering was not accepted, and God warned him of the battle ahead. *"If you do what is right, will you not be accepted? But if you do not do what is right, sin is crouching at your door; it desires to have you, but you must master it."* (Gen 4:7). Perhaps it was just the word 'master', but I was struck with the way this verse connects with the words of Jesus in Matthew 6:24. *"No one can serve two masters. Either he will hate the one and love the other, or he will be devoted to the one and despise the other. You cannot serve both God and money."*

There are all manner of desires that compete with God for that number one spot in our hearts, and for me it was the desire to farm. For many of us, the most common and effective challenger is the desire for money, wealth, possessions, call it what you will. The Greek word translated 'money' in the previous verse is 'mammon', which is not an inanimate object but is more accurately translated as a spirit of money. In the same passage Jesus warns us not to store up treasures on earth, thereby putting our trust and security in wealth and possessions, *"For where your treasure is, there your heart will be also."* (Matt 6:21).

When Richard Foster wrote about the three main temptations in his book, 'Money, Sex and Power', [7] you can see which one he placed first. On a more positive note, Billy Graham once said that, "If a person gets his attitude towards money straight, it will help straighten out almost every other area of his life." [8]

Paul says that, *"The love of money is a root of all kinds of evil. Some people, eager for money, have wandered from the faith and pierced themselves with many griefs."* (1 Tim 6:10). This verse is sometimes misquoted as money being the root of all evil, but that's not what it says. It's the love of money, or the place that money has in our hearts, that is a root of all kinds of evil.

Reading the Gospels I was struck by the crippling effect that a love of money can have on people's hearts and lives. We've already noted the examples of the rich farmer, the rich young man, and Judas, all of whom allowed a love of money and possessions to corrupt their hearts. Jesus tells another parable about a rich man going to hell because he lived in luxury, ignoring the needs of Lazarus, the beggar who lay at his gate (Lk 16:19-31).

---

7   Richard Foster, *'Money, Sex and Power'* Hodder and Stoughton 1985

8   Mark Lloydbottom, *'Blueprint'* published by Your Money Counts 2016 P.25

Jesus gets really angry when he sees the hypocrisy of the temple priests, who have allowed money to rule in their hearts, and so corrupt the Temple worship. The offering of animals for sacrifice could only be carried out if the animals were ritually clean, and the priests sold such animals in the temple courts, but at a price. Their hypocrisy went even deeper when they ruled that these animals could only be bought with 'holy money' i.e the temple shekel, which was available at the money changers tables, at exorbitant rates of exchange. Jesus was livid. He fashioned a whip out of cords and drove the animals out, throwing over the money changers tables and accusing the religious leaders of turning his Father's house into a den of robbers.

In an earlier chapter we noted the sobering story of Ananias and Sapphira in Acts 5. On the face of it, it's a story about two Christians joining in the flow of generous giving that surrounds them, at a time when many in the church were selling land and houses and donating the money to the church to be given to the poor. Ananias and Sapphira sell some property and agree between them that they will keep some of it for themselves, and give only a portion of it to the church's fund for those in need. Nothing wrong with that. It was their money, to do with as they pleased. But for some reason they decide to lie. They pretend they are giving the whole of the amount they got for the property. And God causes them both to drop down dead.

The key to understanding this shocking story is in verse 3. *"Then Peter said, 'Ananias, how is it that Satan has so filled your heart that you have lied to the Holy Spirit and have kept for yourself some of the money you received for the land?"* It's about the heart. All the generous giving around them was coming from the heart, prompted by the love of God. Somehow Ananias and Sapphira allowed Satan to fill their hearts, and in the eyes of God their hearts became rotten. God's response may seem extreme, but it's exactly what we would do if we had a basket of apples and we found a rotten one in the middle. One rotten apple causes the others to go rotten, and God knew the same can happen with our hearts.

Greed is not the only sign of a rotten heart. Jesus rebuked the Pharisees again and again for their arrogance, hypocrisy, self-righteousness, and lack of compassion. They upheld the Law vigorously, tithing even their herbs, but neglected the more important matters of mercy, justice and faithfulness. Typically, in the parable of the Good Samaritan, it was the Priest and the Levite who walked by on the other side. Wherever Jesus ministered, he fought a running battle against cold hearted and hard hearted people, most of whom sadly belonged to the religious establishment.

So much for the bad news. Jesus makes it clear that the answer to being hard hearted or cold hearted is quite simple. Repent and believe. Turn away from, or let go of anything that would capture our hearts, and give our hearts completely to Christ. We need to enthrone Christ as Lord in our hearts, and let go of anything that might get in the way.

The reason he called first the rich young man and then his twelve disciples to '*sell all and give to the poor*' is not because he's advocating some kind of Christian communism. He's just calling his followers to put their trust completely in God, and not to rely for their security on money and possessions. When he commended the poor widow for putting her last two coins into the temple treasury, he was commending her for her faith and absolute trust in God. He wasn't implying that we should not own anything, but that we should hold lightly to everything we have. We don't have to sell, but we do have to surrender. And if we find it hard to surrender, he may call us to sell. If we have already surrendered all we have and are to Christ, then if he prompts us to give something away, we do so, because in surrendering we've already let go of it. We are not to be tight fisted but are called to hold lightly to whatever we've been blessed with, ready to give and to share as the Lord prompts us.

Again, when Jesus sent the disciples two by two ahead of him, and told them not to take a purse or a beggar's bag, he was calling them to rely completely on God, who would provide for all their needs. For many people this total reliance on God seems too extreme, but there is a very good reason for Jesus being so adamant that we must put God first in our hearts, for only then can we be filled with the Holy Spirit. We can either have Jesus ruling in our hearts by his Holy Spirit, or we can have other influences ruling in our hearts. Anything but Jesus will turn us towards selfishness. The only possible way for us to give ourselves to others as Jesus taught, is for our hearts to be completely surrendered to Christ.

To come full circle then, if our giving is decided in the heart, we will only give as God wants if our hearts are completely surrendered to Christ. Many years ago the evangelist D. L. Moody heard someone say, "The world has yet to see what God can do with one man whose heart is totally sold out to God." Moody said to himself, "With God's help, I will be that man." History shows that Moody went on to become the Billy Graham of his generation, travelling the world preaching the Gospel, seeing thousands of people come to Christ. What could that look like in the context of generous giving?

Arguably, in the last two thousand years, there can't be many Christian churches that were more 'sold out to God', than the Early Church in Jerusalem, following the events that took place on the Day of Pentecost. The initial 120 believers were so filled with the Holy Spirit that they poured out into the street, praising God in tongues, and then a further 3,000 people were convicted by the Spirit, baptised into Christ, themselves filled with the Holy Spirit, and joined the church. Today, through reading the book of Acts, we have the privilege of seeing what God can do with thousands of people who are all sold out to God, with their hearts surrendered to Christ and filled with the Holy Spirit. Amongst a daily multitude of miracles and a depth of love beyond our imagining, this is how it affected their capacity to give.

"All the believers were together and had everything in common. Selling their possessions and goods they gave to anyone as he had need... All the believers were one in heart and mind. No one claimed that any of his possessions was his own, but they shared everything they had... there were no needy persons among them. For from time to time those who owned land or houses sold them, brought the money from the sales and put it at the apostles' feet, and it was distributed to anyone as he had need. Joseph (called Barnabas) sold a field he owned and brought the money and put it at the apostles' feet" (Acts 2:44,45; 4:32-37)

Wow. Now we can see why Jesus pushed the boat out when he challenged people to give up anything that might prevent their hearts being totally captivated by God. This is giving that comes from the heart... but only from hearts totally sold out to God. And what's more, the source of that giving is the Holy Spirit. When their hearts were filled with the Holy Spirit, they had a direct connection with God's heart, and the love and grace in the heart of God flowed directly into their hearts in a way they could not contain, so that the same love and grace spilled out to those around them, wherever there was need. Paul speaks of this in his letter to the Romans, where he says, *"God has poured out his love into our hearts by the Holy Spirit, whom he has given us."* (Ro 5 v5).

True Christian giving goes far beyond being kind and generous. It is a grace – a gift from God. And the extent to which we can receive this grace depends largely on the degree to which our hearts are surrendered to Christ. Victory in the battle for the heart leads to an outpouring of grace that will flow into our hearts and through our hearts, flowing out to those in need through practical expressions of compassion and love. Paul challenged the Corinthian church to *"see that you also excel in this grace of giving."* (2 Cor 8:7).

As always, there is a problem, and a very real one at that. The problem for most Christians reading this account is that this level of giving is so beyond our experience, we see it as a mountain that is so high as to be unattainable. We see it as a curiosity of Christian history that despite its power to touch our hearts, has little relevance to the real world, and we move on, touched, stirred, challenged but not changed.

What if we took a different view? What if we stopped and took these verses seriously, and asked, "What can we learn from this, and what can we do as a result?" To begin with, let's grasp the nettle about having *'everything in common'*. The Jerusalem church were in a unique situation. When the crowd reacted to the apostles and others speaking in tongues, there were no less than sixteen different countries or people groups represented (Acts 2:9-11). The 3,000 who were baptised that same day were all part of this crowd. Many of them, quite possibly the majority, were not residents of Jerusalem, but they stayed on in Jerusalem because they were completely overcome by what had happened to them.

"They devoted themselves to the apostles teaching and to the fellowship, to the breaking of bread, and to prayer." (Acts 2 :42). When we read that they broke bread in their homes, the likelihood is that those who were locals welcomed the visitors into their homes, and no doubt gave them accommodation where possible. These visitors were no longer strangers, they had become brothers and sisters in Christ. They were one in heart and mind. They were like family. They weren't just caring for the poor and needy. They were looking after each other. This was truly a unique situation.

That doesn't mean that everything was perfect. In Acts 4:4 we read that the church had grown to over 5,000 people, and was growing daily. In accordance with the culture of the time, the

New Testament authors tended to count men only, which suggests there could well have been ten thousand or more Christians in the Jerusalem church, which represented a huge administrative challenge if everyone was going to be looked after. By Acts 6 we find there were complaints that the Greek-speaking widows were being overlooked in the daily distribution of food, and the church appointed seven deacons to oversee the whole operation properly.

What I'm saying is that this is not the normal situation facing your average church or Christian believer. I don't believe these passages teach us that all Christians should adopt a communist approach to land, houses and possessions. There is no reason to suppose that the early Christians adopted shared ownership as part of their new Christian lifestyle. I would suggest that the more accurate context is that the Jerusalem church were responding to a local humanitarian crisis. In the face of great need around them, many who had property they weren't living in, sold what they could in order to provide for those in need. The need was great, but the response in terms of compassion and generosity was even greater.

This is where the passage becomes relevant, for we have many humanitarian crises in the world today, and sometimes situations on our doorstep that require a radical response. In the UK, more and more churches are now involved with the growing number of Food Banks, which have been set up to help people in poverty, and the Christian charity CAP, which helps people get out of debt and manage their money more responsibly. I write this in 2016, with many countries in Europe facing a situation where millions of Syrian refugees have had to flee their own country due to the ravages and horror of war. They have nowhere to live and no means of support. Some Christians and others have taken refugees into their homes, many churches have organised what help they can for the refugee camps, and many others have donated aid to organisations that are trying to help. These early chapters in the book of Acts challenge us as Christians to respond with compassion and action when we are confronted with great need, and if that means selling some of our possessions in order to help the poor, then so be it.

At the heart of Jesus' teaching on giving was the giving of the heart; a total surrender to Christ, resulting in our hearts being filled with his Spirit, and filled with his love and compassion for people, especially those in need. If we want to give with open hands, then we first need to open our hearts to Christ and to those around us. Open hearts lead to open hands. The greatest example of someone who gave with open hands from an open heart was Jesus himself.

9 Giving and Receiving

harles Swindol tells a heart-warming story about an American soldier based in London at the end of the Second World War. Rationing was still in force, and many families had lost the main provider of the house, leaving them with little or no income, and often hungry and poverty stricken.

"Early one chilly morning an American soldier was making his way back to his barracks in London. As he turned the corner in his jeep, he spotted a little lad with his nose pressed to the window of a pastry shop. Inside the cook was kneading dough for a fresh batch of doughnuts. The hungry boy stared in silence, watching every move. The soldier pulled his jeep to the curb, stopped, got out, and walked quietly over to where the little fellow was standing. Through the steamed-up window he could see the mouth-watering morsels as they were being pulled from the oven, piping hot. The boy salivated and released a slight groan as he watched the cook place them onto a glass-enclosed counter ever so carefully.

The soldier's heart went out to the little boy as he stood beside him. "Son,' he said, 'would you like one of those?" The boy was startled. "Yeah, I would!" he said.

The American stepped inside and bought a dozen, put them in a bag, and walked back to where the lad was standing in the foggy cold of the London morning. He smiled, held out the bag and said, "Here you are." As he turned to walk away, he felt a tug on his coat. He looked back and heard the boy ask quietly, "Mister, are you God?"

Swindol concludes the story by saying, '*We are never more like God than when we give.*' [9]

The Bible says there was one man who had that effect on people all the time. He didn't give doughnuts to one little boy, but he did feed a huge crowd numbering thousands of men, women and children, all of whom were hungry. He wasn't a soldier; he was a carpenter, and his name was Jesus. On one level he was just an ordinary man; on another level he was God in human form, a man who came to show us what God is really like, and how God would give if he were a man. If ever there was a man who gave from the heart, it was Jesus. The one who gave up being God to become a man, and who then gave up his life for ordinary people like you and me.

Paul paints a beautiful picture of Jesus the giver, in the second chapter of his letter to the Philippians. "*Do nothing out of selfish ambition or vain conceit, but in humility consider others better than yourselves. Each of you should look not only to your own interests, but also to the interests of others. Your attitude should be same as that of Christ Jesus:*

Who being in very nature God, did not consider equality with God something to be grasped, but made himself nothing, taking the very nature of a servant, being made in human likeness. And being found in appearance as a man, he humbled himself and became obedient to death - even death on a cross!" (Phil 2:3-8).

Think of the context. John describes Jesus as the 'Word' who was with God from the beginning. He was with God and he was God. All things were created through him. We can imagine him in heaven, enthroned next to the Father, worshipped by the angels, clothed in power and glory, his radiance shining brighter than the noonday sun. And he gives it all up. God so loved the world that

9   Charles Swindol, '*Improving Your Serve*', Hodder and Stoughton 1983. P.52

he gave his only son… And Jesus, in obedience to his Father, gets up from his throne, lays aside his power, his glory, his position in heaven, and humbles himself. He allows himself to be remade, to be born as a tiny, defenceless human baby, born in straw, wrapped in cloth and laid in a manger. Soon to be hunted by an evil king, and taken by his human parents as the child of a refugee family to Egypt.

In today's context of millions of refugees fleeing from the horrors of war in Syria, many of them drowning in the Mediterranean on overcrowded boats, the lucky ones arriving in Europe only to find themselves unwelcome, it's sobering to remember that the God of the Universe chose to enter this world as a defenceless baby in a refugee family.

As if that wasn't enough in showing us the true nature of God, he then humbles himself and takes on the *nature* of a servant. We are so used to the story of Jesus washing the disciples' feet in John 13, we miss the impact of how humiliating it was. Jesus was only half dressed. He was kneeling before them in humility, ready to wash their feet like a shoe shine boy on the streets. The disciples were shocked. Peter said in effect, "You can't do that for me!" (Jn 13:6,8). But this is the true nature of God. He gives himself for us, and he holds nothing back. He gives himself to us, and though like Peter we struggle to receive his grace, he calls us to receive from him and give to others with the same willingness to humbly serve.

What would it look like if we accepted the challenge to have the same attitude as Jesus? What if you and I did nothing out of selfish ambition or vain conceit, but in humility considered others better than ourselves? What if we stopped being concerned only for our own interests, and instead gave ourselves in the interests of others? Is this part of what it means to follow Jesus?

At the age of 30, after decades of quiet obscurity in the backwater village of Nazareth, where no one but his parents had any idea who he really was, Jesus came to be baptised. He committed the rest of his life to obeying his Father in heaven by serving humanity, supremely by giving his life. His father Joseph was already dead, and Jesus as the firstborn in that family would have inherited a double portion of his father Joseph's inheritance, which included a carpentry business as well as the family home, but he gave it all up, leaving his mother in the care of his brothers and sisters, and began travelling and ministering to others. From that day to the day he died his only possessions were the clothes he stood up in.

On the first day of his ministry he called two sets of brothers, Simon and Andrew, and James and John, to leave their fishing business and follow him. That first night he was given hospitality in Simon Peter's home. He began giving and receiving. He healed Peter's Mother-in-law of a fever, and she got up and cooked for him. Wherever he went it was the same; he gave of himself to the crowds as well as to particular individuals, and trusted his Father to prompt at least one person to provide hospitality, including food and a bed for the night. On occasions the Holy Spirit would lead him to that person, as when he called Zacchaeus down from the tree and said "I must stay at your house today." (Lk 19:5).

There were certain families that gave him hospitality whenever he was in the area, such as the two sisters Mary and Martha, and their brother Lazarus. Sometimes Pharisees and others would entertain him, partly out of curiosity, for they were amazed at his teaching and even more so by the healings that seemed to take place every day. It soon got to the point where he gave so much of himself in teaching and healing, that people everywhere gladly welcomed him into their homes, thinking it a great honour even when he came accompanied by twelve disciples, and others besides. Some of those followers also provided, as and where they could. We read that when Jesus hung on the cross, "Many women were there watching from a distance. They had followed Jesus from Galilee to care for his needs." (Matt 27:55).

There were others also who had received ministry from Jesus and then followed him, helping to provide for him and the twelve. *"The Twelve were with him, and also some women who had been cured of evil spirits and diseases; Mary (called Magdalene) from whom seven demons had come out; Joanna the wife of Cuza, the manager of Herod's household; Susanna; and many others. These women were helping to support them out of their own means."* (Luke 8:2,3).

Jesus practised giving and receiving all the time. Every day he gave of himself without holding back, and he was not averse to ask others to give of themselves for his own needs. There are two remarkable occasions during Holy Week. First on Palm Sunday, he tells two of his disciples to go into the village ahead of them, where they would find a donkey tied outside a house. They were to untie the donkey and bring it to him, and if anyone asked what they were doing they were to say, *"The Lord needs it and will send it back here shortly."* (Mk 11:3). When the owners of the donkey heard these words, they gave the donkey gladly.

Again on what we now call Maundy Thursday, he sent Peter and John to go into Jerusalem and follow a water carrier, who would lead them to a certain house, where they were to ask the owner to show them the Upper Room where Jesus and his disciples could celebrate the Passover meal together. It would seem that the Holy Spirit gave Jesus what we would now call a 'Word of Knowledge' about the donkey and the Upper Room, but the point is that Jesus was being led to people who would willingly provide what he needed.

John tells us that as well as those who provided for their needs on a daily basis, the disciples also had a common purse, looked after by Judas (Jn 12:6). They would have used this when Peter and John made preparations for a Passover meal for thirteen, and again in the Samaritan village, when Jesus sat by the well and the disciples went into the village to buy food (Jn 4:8).

This was how Jesus and his disciples lived for three years. Giving of themselves, receiving daily from others, and placing any money they were given into a common purse to share between them. All the time trusting that as they gave themselves to serve the needs of others, so God would provide for their own needs one way or another, usually through other people being prompted to give. Occasionally God provided miraculously, as when Jesus instructed Peter to catch a fish. The fish held in its mouth a four drachma coin, which Jesus then told him to use to pay their temple tax (Matt 17:27).

As they went, Jesus would challenge his disciples to step out in faith on their own, sometimes when he was with them, and sometimes without him. On one occasion he sent out the Twelve to go two by two into the villages ahead of him, proclaiming the Kingdom of God and healing the sick. He specifically told them, *"Do not take along any gold or silver or copper in your belts; take no bag for the journey, or extra tunic, or sandals or a staff; for the worker is worth his keep."* (Matt 10:9,10). Luke tells us that he later sent out seventy-two others with the same instructions.

Jesus taught his disciples to live by faith. They did not get rich, as proponents of the Prosperity Gospel [10] would teach. They focussed on providing for the needs of others, trusting God to provide for their own needs. If the need seemed impossible, then Jesus taught them that nothing is impossible with God, as with the feeding of the five thousand.

And what can we say about him giving up his body and his life, to die for us on the cross? He knew full well it was going to happen, yet he did not hold back. He knew the horror and agony it would entail, and in the Garden of Gethsemane he prayed, *"Father, if*

---

10   See chapter 12 *'Sowing and Reaping'* for a fuller treatment of Prosperity
        Teaching

you are willing, take this cup from me; yet not my will, but yours be done." (Lk 22:42). John tells us, *"Greater love has no one than this, that he lay down his life for his friends."* (Jn 15:13).

The horror of the crucifixion, including the beating and the flogging, enough in itself to bring a man close to death, was not separate from his example of giving. It was the ultimate and supreme demonstration of the fact that Jesus did not just give of himself, he gave all of himself, and held nothing back.

Jesus lived in a perpetual cycle of giving and receiving. To my surprise, one of the biggest lessons on giving that I've learned from Jesus is the importance of receiving. I used to think that Jesus taught, *'Freely give, and freely receive'*. When I looked more closely however, I saw it was the other way round. What he actually said was, *"Freely you have received, freely give."* (Matt 10:8). It was Paul in Acts 20 v35 who quoted Jesus as saying, *"It is more blessed to give than to receive."* I'm not arguing with that, in fact I totally agree, but nevertheless the ability to receive is a huge part of the equation.

Too often in the church we focus on giving to the poor and helping the needy, and forget that if we are going to be truly human, then sometimes we need to let other people give to us. If we are always the givers and not the receivers, we run the danger of presenting ourselves as the dominant partner in the relationship. The one with the more power and the greater resources; the one who is always 'on top', bending down to lift the other one up. In this sort of situation we can too easily assume the moral high ground, and if we're not careful we become condescending and give the impression of being just a little bit superior.

Sometimes it does us good simply to receive. The church in Broad Haven used to give a generous donation to the school next door to the chapel. The reason for that was that quite simply we were indebted to them. The chapel was situated on one side at the end of a very narrow cul de sac, and the school was on the other side. We had no parking at all, but the school had quite a large car park, and they let us use it on a Sunday morning. In fact they let us use it any time out of school hours. It did help that Penny was the school caretaker, holding the keys to the school gates, but it was still very generous of the school to let us use their car park, and we were extremely grateful.

Although in this case we gave a donation to the school every year, there are times when we need to learn to simply receive, without necessarily feeling that we have to give something back in return. How often do neighbours and friends get caught in a cycle of having the same people round for a meal because, 'you invited us last time, so now it's our turn.'

When Paul spoke of the concept of 'giving and receiving', he recognised that it went far wider and deeper than two parties reciprocating with 'one good deed deserves another', or simply returning a favour. Biblically, 'giving and receiving', means giving to one person when they are in need, and then being open to receiving help when we're in need, but not necessarily from the same person. In practice that may mean Barbara helping Sally out when she's in trouble, and then at a later stage, Barbara receiving help from Margaret. Sally may feel indebted to Barbara, and Barbara may feel indebted to Margaret, but as Christians we are all indebted to Jesus, and we repay that debt in some small way by helping whomever the Lord puts in our path. Writing to the Romans, Paul says, *"Let no debt remain outstanding, except the continuing debt to love one another, for he who loves his fellow man has fulfilled the law."* (Ro 13:8).

The danger of returning favours all the time is that we develop a small circle of friends whom we help, while strangers in need can be missed out altogether. This is part of the lesson of Jesus' parable of the Good Samaritan, who stopped and helped a Jew, at a time when there was little love lost between Jews and Samaritans. We need to be ready and willing to help whenever we see the need, but also be ready and open to receiving help ourselves, whenever we are in need.

Paul gives us an example of freely receiving when he says to the church in Philippi, *"It was good of you to share in my troubles... when I set out from Macedonia, not one church shared with me in the matter of giving and receiving, except you only; ... you sent me aid again and again when I was in need... And my God will meet all your needs according to his glorious riches in Christ Jesus."* (Phil 4:14-19).

Paul doesn't say, 'Thanks for your help. I'll pay you back when I can'. He thanks them for their generous help on numerous occasions, and then assures them that when they need help, God will meet their needs by prompting someone to help them, just as they were prompted to help Paul.

We need to learn from Paul's example: the example of someone gratefully receiving help, without feeling they have to 'pay it back'. Like Jesus, Paul knows how to freely receive. He writes, *"I rejoice greatly in the Lord that at last you have renewed your concern for me. Indeed, you have been concerned, but you had no opportunity to show it."* (Phil 4:10)

The phrase 'pay it back' reminds me of a novel I read recently called 'Pay it Forward', by Catherine Ryan Hyde.[11] It's a remarkable novel in which a school teacher gives his class an assignment, challenging them to *"Think of an idea for world change and put it into action'.* Twelve year old Trevor comes up with an inspired idea. He decides to think of a good deed he could do, or rather, three good deeds: one each for three different people.

These are quite significant good deeds. His first idea is to save up his paper-round money and give a hundred dollars to an

---

11   Catharine Ryan Hyde, *'Pay it Forward'*. Black Swan 2007

unemployed person down on their luck, as long as that person could show they would use the money wisely. He puts an advert in the paper, and one homeless man responds by saying if he had a hundred dollars he would buy a new suit which would be a big help when going for a job interview. The man receives his money, buys himself a suit, and gets a job. His life has completely changed around, and he's keen to show his appreciation to his young benefactor. When he tries to pay back the favour however, he gets a surprise.

Trevor's inspired idea is not to 'pay back' but to 'pay it forward'. So he asks the man to think of three people that he could help in some meaningful way, telling him that when these people try to pay him back, he must tell them to pay it forward by helping three others, and so on.

Although it's a fiction, the stories that develop are truly inspirational, and eventually have a significant and positive effect on the community and even the country. Significantly, one of the problems encountered again and again is the problem of persuading needy people to freely receive the help being offered.

When Jesus said, *"Freely you have received, freely give"*, he was talking on two levels. First we need to freely receive the gift of grace and forgiveness which Jesus secured for us on the Cross. Jesus paid the price with his life, and the gift is now freely given, and has to be freely received by faith. Having received this free gift we now need to 'pay it forward' by freely and generously showing grace and forgiveness to others. This is the lesson in his parable of the Unmerciful Servant in Matthew 18:21-35.

A king's servant owes the king a huge debt, almost impossible to pay. But the king has mercy on him and cancels the debt completely. Going out from the king's presence, the servant encounters a colleague who owes him a few quid, or the New Testament equivalent. He demands payment, but his colleague doesn't have any money and promises to pay him back if he will just be patient for a little while. The servant however, has no patience and no mercy. First he violently attacks his colleague, and when that doesn't work, he has him thrown into the debtor's prison. Of course when the king hears what has happened, he is not impressed, to say the least, and has the servant punished.

By contrast, when we realise how much Christ has done for us, then in joyful gratitude we say thank you to Jesus by doing unto others what he has done for us.

That's one level; freely receiving the grace of Christ, and freely giving grace to others. The second level is that we need to freely receive grace from others, and then pay it forward. Not paying back a favour, but allowing one act of kindness to generate other acts of kindness, even to complete strangers. The genius of Hyde's novel is the genius of Christ. I don't know whether it was intentional, but the underlying theme of the story is a wonderful and imaginative modern day adaptation of Jesus' teaching to '*do to others what you would have them do to you.*' (Matt 7:12).

In the novel, as the numbers paying it forward begin to multiply, kindness, grace and mercy begin to spread like wildfire. Not everyone who is helped follows through by paying it forward, because some of us are like the ungrateful servant in Jesus' parable, but lots of people do follow through, and kindness multiplies. I won't spoil the story for you by saying how it ends, but a mass rally of over 20,000 people is held in Trevor's honour, all of whom have been touched by Trevor's concept of paying it forward. The rally is being broadcast on live television with an estimated audience of twenty million. His teacher Reuben challenges the crowd with these words.

"*If Trevor touched your life that much, then maybe you need to pay that forward. In his honour. Twenty million people paying it forward. In a few months, that will be sixty million people. And then a hundred and eighty million.... I know that sounds kind of mind-boggling. But all it really means is that everybody's life would be touched more than once. Three times, six times, someone might pay it forward to you.... We'd all lose track after a while.... It would just keep going around."* [12]

That was the challenge to the crowd. Now here's the challenge to us. Why aren't we doing that in memory of Jesus? This chapter is still about Jesus, even though we've talked a lot about Paul and a fictitious twelve year old boy called Trevor. The point is that all this was inspired by Jesus. He gave his life and told us to do two things. Freely receive, and then pay it forward. If you have received his grace, then pay it forward. Not just three times, but as often as you have the opportunity. And when someone wants to bless you with a random act of kindness, then receive it freely and willingly. The chain of giving is easily broken, and sometimes it's broken by people who won't receive.

The simple idea in Hyde's book has caught on. The book was made into a film, and the film inspired the development of the Pay it Forward Foundation, which sponsors Young Reader editions of the book in schools all over America, spreading the message among the young. Pay it Forward organisations of varying types have been set up in over 75 countries. The UK branch has established an annual Pay it Forward day on April 27th, encouraging people everywhere to carry out 3 random acts of kindness, encouraging the recipients all to pay it forward. As the old saying goes, "You can't give kindness away. It keeps coming back."

Where is the church in all this? Isn't this what we should be doing? Isn't this what Jesus told us to do? Isn't this what we would want to do in memory of Jesus? In honour of his name? Practicing random acts of kindness whenever we have the opportunity?

---

12   Catharine Ryan Hyde, *'Pay it Forward'* Black Swan 2007 P.353

In order for this to happen, we need a change of heart, and a change of heart is exactly what Jesus had in mind when he encountered the religious leaders of his day. Jesus' teaching on giving was radical, and requires a radical change of heart today, just as much as it did then. Part of that radical change of heart is the way we think and feel about people. When God changes our hearts he fills them with love for people. (Ro 5:5).

10 God Loves People

If we were playing word association, and I said, 'people', what other words would come to mind? Crowds? Individuals? Adjectives; like fat people, thin people, rich people, poor people, good people, bad people? If you're an extrovert, the word people might conjure up positive words like party, or team or friends. If you're an introvert, the word people might suggest negative concepts such as traffic jams, crowds of shoppers, noise and nuisance. Some of us love to live in cities where there are lots of people all around; others like to live out in the country where it's peaceful and quiet. How do you like yours? In ones and twos or large groups?

People are funny things. You can love them or loathe them. The German philosopher Arthur Schopenhauer once said that society is like a group of hedgehogs cuddling up close to stay warm. The closer they get, the more they annoy each other with their sharp spines.[13] As human beings we find ourselves in a similar dilemma, sometimes with extreme results, as in the TV programme, 'Neighbours from Hell'. On the other hand, I have a neighbour called Ceri, who's one of the nicest blokes you could meet. A few days after we moved in, I saw him wheeling a barrow round to my shed, but I couldn't ask him what he was doing as

---

13   Arthur Schopenhauer's *Parerga und Paralipomena*, Volume II, Chapter XXXI, Section 396

I was on the phone. The following day he told me he'd dropped some firewood off as he thought we might need some. He would be bringing some more round when he'd finished chopping the logs. Nothing to pay, he said, just being a good neighbour. Some months later he saw me from across the road and called out, "Hello neighbour!" I'd never been called that before, and I have to say it brought a warm feeling to my heart.

God so loved the world. Jesus had compassion for the crowds. He blessed the little children. The lame, the sick, the blind and the lepers, all came to him and he healed them. He ministered to Jews, Samaritans, Romans and Gentiles alike. The fact is, whatever words or names you use, God loves people. He loves them to bits. Every one of them. Enough to die for them. And he wants us to do the same. In fact he once said that if you bundled all of God's laws together and expressed them in one sentence, it would sound something like this: Love the Lord your God and love your neighbour as you love yourself.

By neighbour he didn't just mean the people who live next door, but the person who happens to be in front of you at any given moment, even when you're travelling on the Tube. They might be someone you know well, or perhaps a complete stranger. Whoever it is, God loves them and for this moment in time he has entrusted them into our care. Which means you look out for them and treat them well, you respect them and protect them. Just as you would if you were a grandparent and your daughter asked you to look after the children for the day. Whoever you meet today, friend, family, acquaintance or stranger, is one of God's children and he wants you to look after them.

In today's global world, the word neighbour goes far beyond people we meet day by day. Nowadays we all have the ability to have a positive (or negative) effect on people the other side of the world. Loving our neighbour in the Twenty First Century is about loving our fellow man (or woman) wherever they might be.

I've learned a lot on this journey. There was a time when I'd have said, "What's this got to do with giving?" Now I realise it has everything to do with giving. The Bible's teaching on giving has a definite progression. It starts with *what* you give, the various sacrificial offerings. Like Goldilock's porridge, they had to be 'just right'. The animals had to be ritually clean and unblemished, sometimes the firstborn. Then it was *where*, but not any old where: offerings had to be presented in the Tabernacle, and later in the Temple. With the advent of tithing the *'what and where'* of giving became *how much* and *when*. To be honest, those are still the questions we ask today, especially, 'how much?" That was the question that started me on the journey. How much should I give? How do I work that out?

The Old Testament was quite helpful. It got me as far as tithing the tenth and showed me some good reasons why I should give that much. All well and good. Then along comes Jesus, and all the detail seems to go out the window. How much? What? When? Where? Jesus ignored all that and just said, *"Give, and it will be given to you."* (Lk 6:38). Simple as that. So you could describe it as a principle, a value we should live by, but it's also more than that.

Giving is about people. Giving is about you, God and others, but not in that order. Definitely not that order. It's about God teaching us to put people first. God – people – you… because left to our own devices we don't people first. We always put ourselves first. We need to put God in first place, and then God will teach us to put people first before ourselves.

If that sounds complicated, imagine how I felt about it when I'd just become a Christian in my late teens. While I was still in Agricultural College at Usk, falling in love with Penny and getting to know Jesus at the same time, I read the following words. *"If you want to be my follower you must love me more than your own father and mother, wife and children, brothers and sisters – yes, more than your own life."* (Lk 14:26 NLT).

The bottom line was clear. Jesus was saying that I should love him more than I loved my wife. And as Penny and I had just got engaged, that meant I had to love Jesus more than I loved Penny. For me, that was a problem. I loved Penny 'with all my heart'. I was romantically in love with her in a way I had never been with anyone. The thought of loving Jesus more than I loved Penny just didn't compute. I couldn't get my head round it. Yes, Jesus was my God and I'd asked him to rule in my life, but I couldn't honestly say I loved him more than Penny. Being head over heels in love can really mess with your theology. At the time, I had to accept that this was one of the many things in the Bible I didn't fully understand, and left it at that.

After we'd been married a few years, I came to understand. By that time I had come to realise that no matter how much I loved Penny, no matter how much I put her first before anyone else, the honest fact was that sometimes I couldn't put her first before myself. My love for Penny wasn't always as great as my own selfishness. So when I was milking cows for twelve days at a time and it was my fortnightly weekend off, I didn't always want to go for a day trip with Penny, who was looking forward to spending some quality time with her husband. I much preferred to put my feet up in front of the telly and watch the rugby... which led to a few tense moments and angry words on my weekend off.

Over time I came to see that if I made a deliberate choice to put Jesus first in my life, even before Penny, then actually, Penny would benefit. I started to love Penny not with my own ability, but with the love of Christ. As I put Christ first in my heart, he helped me deal with my selfishness, and helped me to put Penny first before myself. The priority had been me, Penny and then Jesus, but now it had changed to Jesus, Penny and then me.

Husbands and wives reading this might be interested to know that when we both consciously chose to put Jesus first ahead of each other, a remarkable thing happened. Jesus helped me to see that

I needed to spend quality time with Penny on our weekend off, and at the same time he helped Penny to see that after working for twelve days, on my weekend off I needed time to relax. Between us, and with a lot of help from above, we worked it out.

I'd learned an important lesson. God first, others second, me last. And then I learned another lesson: putting others before ourselves is not about putting us down. It's about lifting others up; giving them more respect and a higher value than perhaps we'd given them before. But that doesn't mean we disrespect or devalue ourselves. What Jesus was trying to teach me (and it took a while to learn) is that he valued me beyond my imagining, he wanted me to really value myself, and then he wanted me to value others the same way. That's what he meant when he said, "*Love your neighbour as you love yourself*." Think about your neighbour the way you think about yourself. Value your neighbour the way you value yourself.

For some of us that might be a problem. Many of us unfortunately don't value ourselves very highly. We put ourselves down. Some of us simply don't like ourselves. We imagine that other people see us the same way we see ourselves, and that they don't like us either.

I used to have a colleague who was a Christian youth worker. He regularly taught the youth that God loved them, but one day he confided in me that he wasn't sure how much that applied to him. "I know God loves me,' he said, 'but I'm not sure that he likes me." I tried to assure him that the fact that God loved him also meant that God actually liked him. A lot. I encouraged him to make a practice of looking in the mirror and saying to himself, "I like you. I respect you. I value you." I'm not sure if it worked for him, but it certainly worked for me. I wouldn't have been able to do it on my own, but over the years I learned that God loved me and liked me. He even respected me. I knew that because he gave me free will, and he refused to take it away from me.

If God loved me, then I could learn to love myself. And if I could learn to love myself, then I could learn to love, value and respect others in the same way. I was gradually learning what it means to *'love your neighbour as you love yourself'*.

As I continued on my journey through the Bible I learned yet another lesson; this time about being a servant. One of my favourite passages is Philippians 2:1-11, where Paul focusses on our attitude to others, and then puts the spotlight on Jesus himself. What struck me one day was that when Jesus emptied himself of his glory in heaven, humbled himself, made himself nothing and became a man, he then took on himself *'the very nature of a servant.'* He didn't just serve occasionally, as when he washed the disciples' feet, he made it his nature. His calling. John tells us that Jesus did not come to condemn the world but to save the world (Jn 3:17), and he did that by serving. By making himself our slave, even to the extent of dying for us on the Cross. He didn't become a servant in the sense that he did everything we wanted or ordered. But he did everything we needed, and one thing we needed was to learn to value and respect both ourselves and those around us.

I've still got a long way to go, but I was challenged by what it meant to take on the nature of a servant. Could it be that God had put me on this earth to serve others? To attend to their needs, to look after people, to make sure they're well fed and clothed? To shift my focus from looking after 'number one' to looking after others?

The worship leader and song writer Graham Kendrick put it like this. *"This is our God, the Servant King. He calls us now to follow him... So let us learn how to serve, and in our lives enthrone him; each other's needs to prefer, for it is Christ we're serving."*[14]

---

14   Graham Kendrick, *'The Servant King'*. Copyright 1983 Make Way Music

When I consider the real world and what some people are like, I sometimes struggle with this. Would I really want to serve him? Or her? Or them? And then I remember another lesson about grace.

Grace basically means that God loves us and does things for us even when we least deserve it. As when Jesus called a mean, cheating, unscrupulous tax collector like Zacchaeus down out of his tree, went home to have tea with him and showed him so much love and grace that Zacchaeus' hard heart melted. He began to see the people he had used and cheated in a new way and said, *"Look Lord, here and now I give half of my possessions to the poor, and if I have cheated anybody out of anything, I will pay back four times the amount."* (Lk 19:8).

It's all about people. When God created the world, he finished the work with one final *piece de resistance*. He made people, just like himself. In fact the whole earth and even the universe was made for them. For people, like you and me. And when things went wrong and the people messed up, he sent Jesus. He gave his son for the sake of... people. So when Jesus taught about giving, he wasn't teaching theology or doctrine, he was looking at people. People who needed to be loved and cared for.

A young nun went to work with Mother Theresa, helping the poor in the slums of Calcutta. One day an emaciated beggar was brought in off the streets. He was filthy, covered in fleas and lice, had foul smelling pus weeping from open sores, and he stank, partly because he'd been drinking and had just vomited all over himself. He was very weak and could hardly stand. The young nun was assigned to give the beggar a bath, but she just couldn't bring herself to touch him, let alone bathe him. Mother Theresa stepped in and bathed him herself. Afterwards, feeling ashamed, the nun apologised to Mother Theresa and asked her how she could bring herself to show such care and tenderness to such filthy beggars. Mother Theresa did not reproach her, but told the nun she'd had similar struggles herself when she was younger.

Since then, she said, she had learned to look at people a different way. She had learned to look at people, whoever they were, rich or poor, and see Jesus. She would think of Jesus, imagining him just after he'd been beaten and flogged, and then she would care for the person, in whatever way was appropriate, just as she would care for Jesus. Jesus, the one who welcomes the faithful into his Kingdom with the words,

"For I was hungry and you gave me something to eat, I was thirsty and you gave me something to drink, I was a stranger and you invited me in, I needed clothes and you clothed me, I was sick and you looked after me, I was in prison and you came to visit me... Whatever you did for one of the least of these, you did for me." (Matt 25:35,36,40)

Of course we can't all be like Mother Theresa. But imagine the difference it would make throughout the world if we all thought more about other people than ourselves. In one sense, it's the difference between heaven and hell.

The story is told of a huge table in hell, full of sumptuous food. The table is surrounded by hungry people, but there is more than enough food for everyone, and everyone is allowed to eat to their hearts content. There are however, certain rules which must be adhered to strictly. First, everyone must use the spoons provided. Second, the spoons must be held at the end of the handle. It all sounds simple enough, until we realise that the handles are five foot long. As a result, hell is full of starving people desperately trying to feed themselves, but who cannot do so because no matter how hard they try, they just cannot bring the food to their mouths. So near, and yet so far. Hell indeed.

In this story, the picture of heaven is almost identical. The same huge table covered with sumptuous food and surrounded by hungry people; the same spoons with five foot handles, and exactly the same rules. But in heaven there is a fundamental difference.

In heaven they are all well fed and content. Why? Because in heaven they feed each other. They follow the same rules but they also follow the Golden Rule laid down by Jesus. To do unto others as you would have them do unto you (Matt 7:12).

There are three simple steps to Christian giving. Invite Jesus to rule in your heart and fill you with his Spirit. Learn to love yourself, and to love people as you love yourself. And then give to others whatever they need, whenever God prompts you.

PART 4

PAUL TEACHES GRACE
AND BLESSING

11 The River of Grace

" **T**here is a river whose streams make glad the city of God, the holy place where the Most High dwells." Psalm 46:4

There is a river that flows right through the Bible, from Genesis to Revelation. It is usually referred to as the River of Life, but I would suggest we can see it also as a river of grace. In Genesis 2 we read of the Garden of Eden, sometimes called Paradise. It was a place of beauty and peace; a place where God walked in the cool of the evening; a place where man and woman walked with God. The Bible tells us there was something in particular which gave life to that garden and sustained it. "*A river watering the garden flowed from Eden*". (Gen 2:10).

We see the same river in Ezekiel 47, where water flows out from under the altar in the Temple. The water continues to flow, becoming knee deep, waist deep, and then deep enough to swim in; a river so wide that no one could cross. Trees grow on either side of the river, bearing fruit of all kinds; where it empties into the sea, the salt water becomes fresh; the river brings life wherever it flows.

The source of this river is Jesus himself, who makes it possible for all who believe, to drink of this water of life. The apostle John records Jesus coming to the Temple in Jerusalem at the Feast of Tabernacles. "*On the last and greatest day of the feast, Jesus stood up and said in a loud voice, 'If anyone is thirsty, let him come to me and drink. Whoever believes in me, as the Scripture has said, streams of living water will flow from within him. By this he meant the Spirit, whom those who believed in him were later to receive."* (Jn 7:37-39).

In the very last chapter of the Bible, the Garden of Eden has been replaced by the City of God, but the same river flows through the city. *"Then the angel showed me the river of the water of life, as clear as crystal, flowing from the throne of God and of the Lamb down the middle of the great street of the city. On each side of the river stood the tree of life, bearing twelve crops of fruit, yielding its fruit every month. And the leaves of the trees are for the healing of the nations."* (Rev 22:1,2).

As the last chapter of the Bible draws to its close, the Spirit and the bride, the redeemed people of God, cry out together saying, *"Come! Whoever is thirsty, let him come; and whoever wishes, let him take the free gift of the water of life."* (Rev 22:17).

This is not an exposition of the biblical picture of the River of Life, but the free gift of the water of life is very much part of the river of grace that we have been following in our journey together. I want to use this analogy of the river to guide us through Paul's deep and profound teaching on the grace of giving in Chapter 8 of his second letter to the Corinthians.

The context is that the church in Jerusalem and Judea was not only poor, but also suffering the effects of famine, leading to great hardship. As Paul journeyed around the Gentile churches he urged them to help their brothers and sisters in Judea by giving generously to an organised appeal which would be taken to Jerusalem by trusted members of the church (Acts 11:27-30). Corinth had previously promised to give to this appeal, and in 2 Corinthians he urges them to make good their promise, citing the generosity of the churches in Macedonia to encourage them in their giving.

Not far from where we live, near Talybont in Breconshire, are the Blaen y Glyn Waterfalls. A fast flowing river cascades down a steep valley, resulting in spectacular waterfalls falling headlong into deep pools which then overflow with water, causing more rushing waterfalls to repeat the process again and again as the river flows swiftly down the valley. As we look together at 2 Corinthians Chapter 8, I want us to imagine a river rushing down a steep valley, causing waterfalls to cascade into deep pools which then overflow, causing more waterfalls and pools further downstream. It may sound poetic, but I hope you will catch the sense of the river of grace that flows headlong from God to the church, and on to those in need. It's a picture echoing the language of Malachi, where God promises to throw open the floodgates of heaven, and pour out so much blessing we will not have room enough for it.

"And now brothers, we want you to know about the grace that God has given the Macedonian churches." (2 Cor 8:1).

Grace is sometimes spelled God's Riches At Christ's Expense. All good things come from God, and they come direct to us through faith in the sacrifice of Christ on the Cross. They cannot be earned or in any way deserved. They are gifts freely given from a God who loves to give. As Paul prepares to tell of the wondrous generosity of the Macedonian church, he recognises that their ability to give so generously is itself a gift from God. When we read of the amazing situation in Acts 2, where new Christians sold land and possessions to give to the poor, this is very much the result of Christians who have been filled with the Holy Spirit, changing their hearts and filling them with faith and compassion. In his letters to the churches in Rome and Corinth, Paul wrote in depth of the gifts or spiritual abilities which the Holy Spirit gives to the people of God. Included in these varied gifts is the gift of generosity (Ro 12:8). This pouring out of God's grace into the hearts of his people is the first waterfall, causing a deep pool of joy which itself overflows.

"Out of the most severe trial, their overflowing joy and their extreme poverty welled up in rich generosity." (2 Cor 8:2).

When Paul spoke of extreme poverty he meant just that. The severe trial was doubtless some form of persecution against the church, something that Paul himself encountered on a regular basis. These two factors together, and in particular their extreme poverty, would be enough to stop most people from even thinking of giving to others, but in this case they are countered by this deep pool of joy, continually fed by the waterfall of grace being poured into their hearts by the Holy Spirit, and their joy overflows. It wells up; it can't be held back; it overflows and itself becomes a roaring waterfall of rich generosity. And again, when Paul spoke of rich generosity, he meant exactly that. These impoverished Christians gave so generously, that Paul himself was completely taken aback.

"For I testify that they gave as much as they were able, and even beyond their ability." (2 Cor 8:3).

From a human point of view, being in extreme poverty, they were simply not able to give. No one can give what they haven't got. But actually, everyone has something. It's just that before we even start to think about giving to others, we automatically think first of what we need for ourselves. We work out our own needs, and then consider whether we have anything left to give away. In cases of extreme poverty these sums don't take long to work out. But we're forgetting about the sheer power of the waterfall feeding this particular pool. Part of the grace being poured into their hearts was a potent mixture of faith and compassion. Love for God and love for others. They had every faith that if they gave to others in need, God would look after their own needs. And their compassion was so strong they would have given anyway, even without the faith that God would provide. Despite their own poverty and persecution, they were full of God's love for the needy, and they just couldn't help but give generously.

Some years ago I stood alongside the mighty Niagara Falls, trying to calculate in my own mind the sheer volume of water flowing over those thunderous falls. The total liquid amount in gallons or litres passing over the top every second was mind blowing. What was even more incredible was the sheer quantity of water behind, enabling that immense waterfall to keep going 24 hours a day for weeks, months and even years on end. The Macedonians were not relying on their own resources when they gave with rich generosity. They were relying in faith on the sheer quantity that flowed daily in God's river of grace.

"Entirely on their own, they urgently pleaded with us for the privilege of sharing in this service to the saints." (2 Cor 8:4).

When you see a waterfall cascading over the rocks, you sense the exuberance, the noise, the sheer power and the excitement. For the Macedonians their faith was exciting. Despite their physical poverty they were living in spiritual abundance. And part of that abundance was the joy of giving. It gave them a buzz. They were more than just cheerful givers, they loved to give. As golfers love to golf, and football fans love to cheer on their team, these people loved to give. Not to give would have meant missing out in a way that would have caused deep disappointment, like missing the final at Wimbledon. For this reason they pleaded for the opportunity to give. It was not a duty but a privilege. One they enjoyed immensely.

"And they did not do as we expected, but they gave themselves first to the Lord and then to us in keeping with God's will." (2 Cor 8:5)

We shall look at this verse in more detail later on, as different people interpret it in different ways. But however we interpret the detail, the fact is that they gave themselves wholly and unreservedly to God AND to the needy. The more evangelical wing of the church is sometimes guilty of giving themselves to God, but holding back when it comes to caring for others. Those who belong more to the liberal wing of the church may throw themselves into helping the poor and needy, but are sometimes accused of not being so completely committed to God. The sheer power of the grace given to the Macedonians is such that both these strands are caught up together in the rushing waters of this river of grace.

"So we urged Titus, since he had earlier made a beginning, to bring also to completion this act of grace on your part." (2 Cor 8:6)

It's one thing to read about, think about, and even talk about grace. But grace is not completed until it becomes an act. The grace of our Lord Jesus Christ is not a theological concept. It was a human act of sacrifice carried out on a certain day by a real person in a real place at a definite point in history. Likewise the Corinthians' promise to give to the Judean appeal meant nothing until it was completed. The very tone of Paul's letter suggests they needed some encouragement to bring their earlier promise to completion. And it could only be completed by an act. The act of giving. The Good Samaritan is not remembered for his fine convictions and principles. He is remembered for what he did. If when this book is read and digested, it does not lead to action, then what's the point? Without action the work of grace is not complete. The river of grace is not static. It flows; it rushes headlong over the waterfall; it pours down into the pool below; it overflows to the next level; it never stops till it comes to the sea, and even then it is caught up in an energy far greater than its own. Jesus did not encourage us to consider the example of the Good Samaritan. He said to go and DO likewise.

"But just as you excel in everything – in faith, in speech, in knowledge, in complete earnestness and in your love for us – see that you also excel in this grace of giving." (2 Cor 8:7)

The Corinthian church were known for their love of spiritual gifts, but not always for their love for each other. Paul had to rebuke them for the way they practised the Lord's Supper, which in those days was a full meal. Those who arrived early had a tendency to eat and drink to their hearts content, leaving nothing for those who came later. The latecomers would often be servants or slaves who had to work late before they could come to church. *"When you come together, it is not the Lord's Supper you eat, for as you eat, each of you goes ahead without waiting for anybody else. One remains hungry, another gets drunk."* (1 Cor 11:20,21). Earlier in the same letter he had to rebuke them for the quarrelling, jealousy and division within the church. (1 Cor 3:3,4)

When Paul praises the church for the way they excel in various spiritual gifts, and then urges them to excel in the grace of giving, he is not merely encouraging them to add yet another gift to their portfolio of spiritual gifts. He is encouraging them to do something which will change their attitude to each other and to others in a profound, positive and life changing way. Our attitude to giving to the needs of others is absolutely fundamental to our Christian faith and practice. It affects everything we do.

For over 30 years I have practiced the gifts of speaking in tongues, prophecy, and healing. I do so with deep gratitude to God who gives good gifts to his children (I'm not very proficient, but I do practice!). I have been at many conferences and seminars where there has been teaching on particular gifts and then encouragement and help to enable people to receive those gifts. All well and good. I personally believe we need all the help we can receive to live the Christian life. The Holy Spirit is our guide and our helper, and we should not shrink back from any help he can give us.

The problem is we tend to pick and choose. Thousands of believers all over the world have prayed and longed for the gifts of speaking in tongues and healing, but how many of us pray and long for the gift of generosity, or the gift of mercy, both named in Paul's list of spiritual gifts in Romans 12:8? To excel in the grace or gift of giving, we need to give where and when we can, as the Bible teaches and our hearts prompt us, and we need to ask the Holy Spirit to help us do this more and more. Or we can start by asking for the gift of generosity, as long as we don't sit around waiting for it to drop out of the sky. I have learned enough over the years to know that when we ask God for some spiritual gift or ability, we then need to step out in faith believing that God has already given us that gift. The ability comes as we step out in faith.

To excel in the grace of giving can be more than a challenge. Why not make it your dream; your ambition; your desire. Do you think God would want you to have a desire like that? Is there any reason why he wouldn't? Can you think of anything else at this present time which would help you to be more Christ-like? If you allowed this river of grace to pour unhindered into the pool of your heart, can you begin to imagine what might overflow?

"I am not commanding you, but I want to test the sincerity of your love by comparing it with the earnestness of others." (2 Cor 8:8)

Sincerity has not always been seen as the hallmark of the Church. How often did Jesus rebuke the Jewish religious leaders for their hypocrisy? Many people in today's secular society view churchgoers as hypocrites. They may not be right, but sadly over the years there has been enough evidence here and there to confirm them in this view.

What if they began to see evidence of a different kind? What if they saw concrete evidence of such sincerity and generosity of heart, that they wrote letters to the local church, as happened at Broad Haven, expressing their admiration of the church's 'truly Christian attitude"?(see Chapter 14). Wouldn't it be wonderful if the tide began to change, and Christians everywhere became known for their sincere love and generosity? It happened in the early church. The outside world looked at the Christian church almost in disbelief and exclaimed, *"See how they love one another!"*

With regard to sincerity, I'm aware that some of my readers will be asking, "How does this tie in with Jesus' command not to let the left hand know what the right hand is doing?" (Matt 6:3). This is where sincerity comes in. We do not give in order to be praised, and we will often give completely in secret, but the fact is that if this is the state of our hearts, then sooner or later it will be noticed, no matter how much we try to hide it. Jesus calls us to live such lives that we become like lights to a dark world, leading people to see God as he really is. *"Let your light shine before men, that they might see your good deeds and praise your Father in heaven."* (Matt 5:16).

"For you know the grace of our Lord Jesus Christ, that though he was rich, yet for your sakes he became poor, so that you through his poverty might become rich." (2 Cor 8:9).

This is where the mere trickle of our own grace becomes a raging torrent in Christ. Paul goes far beyond the amazing example of the Macedonian church to the example of Christ himself. Above all else Jesus was known for his grace. To come to Jesus is to come to the very source of the river of grace. To put our faith in Christ is to drink of this living water. And to follow Christ in showing love to others is to experience this river of grace flowing from him, through ourselves, and on to others.

Jesus never asked anyone to do what he wasn't prepared to do himself. When he sent the disciples out two by two and told them to take no money with them but to trust God to provide, that's exactly what Jesus did every day for three years. And when he told the rich young man to sell all and give to the poor, and then follow Christ in trust and obedience, that's exactly what Jesus did, and more. He gave up his throne in heaven; his power and glory and the worship of the angels; he laid it all down in order to humble himself and take on the nature of a servant. He came down to earth as a mortal human being and became obedient to his Father, trusting his Father to provide for his daily needs.

In love he gave his body for us on the Cross, causing a mighty waterfall of grace to flow with such power and quantity that two thousand years later the river still flows. The old Welsh revival hymn, 'Here is love', sums it up beautifully:

'On the mount of crucifixion,

Fountains opened deep and wide;

Through the floodgates of God's mercy,

Flowed a vast and gracious tide.

Grace and love, like mighty rivers,

Poured incessant from above;

And heaven's peace and perfect justice,

Kissed a guilty world in love.' [15]

To bring things down to a human level, let me turn from a river to a tap. When I was a boy, milking cows in my father's cowshed, we washed the shed by filling a bucket of water from a tap. I would throw the bucket of water across the concrete floor and then brush it with a stiff yard brush. Nowadays I do some relief milking on a farm with 550 cows, milked in a huge milking parlour. A bucket of water wouldn't go far in that situation, so we use a high volume pressure washer. I simply turn on the tap, aim the pressure washer where I need it, and the water just keeps flowing.

Where giving is concerned you and I can choose to be 'bucket givers' or 'hosepipe givers'. 'Bucket givers' think of themselves as only having a limited amount available, so they give sparingly. 'Hosepipe givers' give generously, even extravagantly, because they know that as long as the tap is turned on, they will never run out of water. When we give generously to others, we can know

---

15   *'Here is Love'* William Rees

that God's amazing river of grace will never, ever, run out. God gives to us so that we can give to others, and as we keep giving to others, so God will keep giving to us. *"And God is able to make all grace abound to you, so that in all things at all times, you will abound in every good work."* (2 Cor 9:8)

12 Sowing and Reaping

B lessing is not the same as grace. In fact, there's a really important distinction. Grace is something given, that is neither earned nor deserved in any way. Christ's death on the Cross, and all it achieved for those who believe, was grace. The forgiveness, peace with God, and eternal life that comes to us through faith in Christ can never be earned or deserved. When you buy someone a present simply because you want to give them something, that's grace.

The problem with the word blessing, rather like the word love, is that it can have different meanings in today's language. So for instance if Penny and I as grandparents want to bless our grandchildren, we might buy them a present. Biblically speaking that's grace, because it wasn't earned or deserved, but today we would say that we wanted to bless them. In the Bible the word blessing can also have different meanings, but the usual understanding was that blessing was earned or deserved in some way. In direct contrast to grace, blessing was often given as a reward. One of the first great examples of blessing in the Bible is when God blesses Abraham and tells him his descendants would one day become a nation. *"I swear by myself, declares the Lord, that because you have done this and not withheld your son, your only son, I will surely bless you and make your descendants as numerous as the stars in the sky and as the sand on the seashore."* (Gen 22:16,17).

This blessing was not given out of undeserved grace. Abraham had been tested. He passed the test by being obedient and showing he was willing to sacrifice anything for God, even his beloved son. We know that God never intended him to do this, but the fact is that Abraham was rewarded *'because you have done this'*, and the reward took the form of a great blessing.

When the Israelites were commanded to tithe, they were promised that if they were obedient in tithing, then God would bless them. They were told to tithe, *"so that the Lord your God may bless you in all the work of your hands."* (Dt 14:29). The whole of Deuteronomy 28 conveys the message that obedience to the law will result in blessing, whereas disobedience will bring a curse. *"All these blessings will come upon you and accompany you if you obey the Lord your God."* (Dt 8:2).

Again and again throughout the Bible, God promises to bless his people if they will obey him. So for instance, Proverbs 3:9,10 says, *"Honour the Lord with your wealth, with the firstfruits of all your crops; then your barns will be filled to overflowing, and your vats will brim with new wine."*

As Christians we might be forgiven for thinking that blessing as a reward for obedience is an Old Testament concept, that no longer applies under the new covenant of grace. Jesus however, makes it clear that this is not the case. Three times in his Sermon on the Mount, when he is encouraging his hearers to give, pray and fast, he says, *"Then your Father, who sees what is done in secret, will reward you."* (Matt 6:4,6,18).

Jesus' command to give, although not limited to a tenth, makes it very clear that obedience in this matter will result in great blessing, *"Give and it will be given to you. A good measure, pressed down, shaken together and running over, will be poured into your lap. For with the measure you use, it will be measured to you."* (Lk 6:38). With this last sentence Jesus takes the concept of blessing as a reward even further, stating clearly that the amount of blessing will be in direct correlation with the amount we give. Paul repeats this principle with the analogy of sowing and reaping.

"Remember this: Whoever sows sparingly will also reap sparingly, and whoever sows generously will also reap generously." (2 Cor 9:6).

I learned this to my cost when I was farming. In the early eighties I spent two years on a farm near Leominster, and on one occasion I had to sow a field with kale, which is a sort of big leaved cabbage on long stalks grown for cattle. The kale seed is tiny and was spread with a fertiliser spinner. In other words it wasn't planted directly into the ground but broadcast by machine. Sowing the seed this way was not very exact and it was easy to miss some of the ground, so I was told to sow the seed twice. First up and down the field, and then across the field. Driving the tractor up and down the field was fine, even though it was rather steep at one point. But driving the tractor across the steep area was a different matter altogether. I was employed as a herdsman and had never been an expert tractor driver. Part of the steep slope was concave in shape, which made the top part very steep indeed, and driving across it gave me the distinct impression that the tractor could roll over at any moment, so to be on the safe side I missed out the very steep part. After all, I thought, I've sown it up and down, so it won't matter if I miss some of it out when I'm going across.

The field sloped upwards from the main road, and a few months later what I'd done was obvious to every passing farmer. The field was covered with a thick luxuriant crop of kale, except for a narrow strip across the steep area, where the crop looked decidedly thin. I was instantly reminded of Paul's words about sowing sparingly and reaping sparingly. I had learned to my cost that this is a principle embedded in the laws of nature.

It is also a spiritual principle, and that principle works both ways. *"Sow generously and you will also reap generously."* The two most important words in verse 6 are those two little words which we so often pass over and hardly notice. *"REMEMBER THIS."* Paul is emphasising the point that what he's about to say is really, really important. In the same way that Jesus would often say, *"Truly, truly, I say unto you."* Jesus always spoke the truth, but there were times when he was basically saying, 'Sit up and listen up. This is really important!" Paul is saying that his phrase about sowing and reaping is more than a simple analogy. It's a biblical principle that we need to take note of, and it's a principle that applies particularly to our giving, as we see in Proverbs 11:24,25. *"One man gives freely, yet gains even more; another withholds unduly, but comes to poverty. A generous man will prosper; he who refreshes others will himself be refreshed."*

The more we respond to God in trust and obedience, the more God will pour out his blessing. This is not grace, which cannot be earned, this is the reward of blessing, poured out in response to obedience and faith.

I need to emphasise, and say as clearly as I can, that this blessing in response to obedience is NOT what some people call 'Prosperity Teaching', also referred to as 'Health, Wealth and Prosperity'.

Prosperity teaching, which has become very popular in some denominations and countries, builds on everything that I have already said about the reward of blessing, but then interprets and applies this in a way that encourages Christians to focus on themselves, rather than others, with the emphasis on blessing the preacher's ministry, and/or themselves, rather than the poor. Prosperity teaching begins with the scriptural truth that God blesses those who give, but the twist comes in the motivation. Instead of the motive being to bless others, and God encouraging and enabling that desire, the motive becomes being blessed ourselves, and that applies both to the preacher and the congregation.

The change of emphasis is ever so slight, but the results are catastrophic. The basic theme is, obey God by giving to the preacher's church and/or ministry, and God will bless YOU with health, wealth and prosperity. The teaching is backed up by quoting verses such as, *"He who trusts in the Lord will prosper."* Or

"Misfortune pursues the sinner, but prosperity is the reward of the righteous." (Prov 28:25; 13:21).

There are many other such verses we could quote, but the problem is that quoting these verses on their own doesn't tell the whole story. If we don't tell the whole story we could make a convincing case biblically from Genesis 22 that God commands his people to sacrifice their firstborn sons. We could then back up our case by quoting verses on tithing which state that the firstborn belongs to the Lord. Heresy always starts with an element of truth, but then fails to tell either the whole truth, or nothing but the truth.

Imagine an engineer making a slight miscalculation when laying railway tracks, so that instead of being exactly parallel, the end of one track is just millimetres further away from the other track than it should be. Further down the line the gap between the tracks will become wider and wider, until the train is derailed.

In Prosperity Teaching, verses such as, *'You will be made rich in every way'* (2 Cor 9:11), are taken completely out of context, ignoring the fact that no Christian leader in the New Testament ever became rich. Paul writes to Timothy and asks him to bring the cloak that Paul left at Troas, presumably because that was the only one he owned (2 Tim 4:13). Jesus himself, when he died on the cross, owned only the clothes he stood up in. It is true that Old Testament kings like David and Solomon were blessed with riches and great wealth, but that was because in their role as king they represented the nation, and the wealth of the king represented God's blessing on the nation as a whole.

The really sad thing about such heresies is that honest sincere Christians wanting to follow Christ can be taken in with this teaching, and in doing so they allow their hearts to become contaminated, and end up serving mammon instead of serving God. The Lausanne Theology Working Group produced a statement on Prosperity Teaching in October 2008. [16] This is their definition and response to Prosperity Teaching.

"We define prosperity gospel as the teaching that believers have a right to the blessings of health and wealth and that they can obtain these blessings through positive confessions of faith and 'sowing of seeds' through the faithful payments of tithes and offerings [...]

It is our overall view that the teachings of those who most vigorously promote the 'prosperity gospel' are false and gravely distorting of the Bible, that their practice is often unethical and unChristlike, and that the impact on many churches is pastorally damaging, spiritually unhealthy, and not only offers no lasting hope, but may even deflect people from the message and means of eternal salvation."

However, having rejected the heresy of Prosperity Teaching, we must be careful not to throw the baby out with the bath water. The biblical truth of blessing and reward still remains, and in the New Testament Jesus gets to the heart of what it's all about. Basically, God wants to help and provide for people in need, but he doesn't parachute aid directly from heaven. Instead he prompts his own people, both the church in general and individual Christians in particular, to respond generously whenever they come across need. To enable us to continue in this ministry, God gives to those who give, in order that they can keep on giving. The motive for the giver is to bless others, and if the motive and action is right, then God will continue to bless the giver so that others can be blessed.

"Each man should give what he has decided in his heart to give, not reluctantly or under compulsion, for God loves a cheerful giver." (2 Cor 9:7).

---

16   Lausanne Theology Working Group, 'A *Statement on Prosperity Teaching'*. Quoted in Christianity Today, Dec 8th 2009

I would imagine that if Christians were polled on their favourite biblical verse about giving, this would surely come out on top. We love this verse because of the freedom it brings. Freedom from rules; freedom from guilt; freedom from having to do whatever your local church or preacher says; freedom to make up your own mind in any and every situation; freedom from any pressure. So much freedom in fact, that giving actually becomes something we can enjoy, and discover at last what it means to be a cheerful giver. It might interest you to know that the Greek word translated 'cheerful' is actually *hilaron*, from which we get our English word 'hilarious'. What's more, God approves. God loves a hilarious giver.

Before we get carried away with too much hilarity, I'm afraid I have to be a party pooper. In reality, the reason why this verse is so popular in our churches, is that many people interpret it as meaning they can give as little as they like, and God will still approve. Like God approving of Cain's offering rather than Abel's. That hardly seems likely, in light of the fact that Paul has been encouraging these very people to *'see that you also excel in this grace of giving.'* In verse 5 he talks about finishing the arrangements for *'the generous gift you had promised'*.

Contrary to popular opinion, this verse does not give freedom to give as little as we like, in fact it does the opposite. Paul is giving them absolute freedom to give as MUCH as they want. And what's more they can give as much as they want without any sense of reluctance, because no matter how much they give, they're not going to lose out. In fact they will gain. And there's no compulsion either. Paul doesn't have to wave a stick because he's just waved a carrot. He's just told them that the more generously they sow, the more generously they will reap. And then he waves another carrot...

"And God is able to make all grace abound to you, so that in all things at all times, having all that you need, you will abound in every good work." (2 Cor 9:8).

When we sow generously we reap generously, but that reaping may take many different forms and come in all shapes and sizes. Having all that you need to abound in every good work may include having an opportunity you didn't have before; having the time to do it; as well as having the health, skill, energy, money, and whatever resources may be needed. Danielle Strickland, a Salvation Army Major, evangelist and international conference speaker, once told an amazing story of how God provided everything she needed for a good work that she didn't even know God wanted her to do, until it happened. [17]

After yet another speaking engagement, Danielle arrived at an airport in Ukraine, ready to fly home. She already had her ticket bought and paid for, so she was quite happy to use the last of her cash to pay the taxi driver, before walking into the airport. There she found that her flight had been cancelled, and the next one was not due for another three days! "Now what do I do?" she thought, "I've got no money. I don't know anyone. I've got nowhere to stay. And I'm stuck here for three days!"

Not surprisingly, she sat down and prayed, then opened her Bible to see what God might say. As she leafed through her Bible, she was rather surprised to find a ten dollar bill, sitting between the pages of her Bible. She hadn't put it there and she didn't know where it came from, but there it was, so she said a prayer of thanks, and decided to use the money to pay the bus fare into the city, thinking she might find a Salvation Army hostel, where she could stay for the next three days.

---

17   Danielle Strickland, speaking at New Wine, Shepton Mallet. August 2016

The bus fare was exactly ten dollars. She paid the fare and sat down in the only spare seat available, next to a smartly dressed man in a suit. Being an evangelist, she said hello, and soon engaged the man in conversation. Almost immediately he said, "You are a Christian! You can tell me about God!" Over the course of a long bus ride, she talked about God, responded to the man's questions, and led him to Christ, just before he got off at his usual stop. She had thought he might suggest somewhere she could stay, but he just thanked her profusely and got off the bus.

Twenty minutes later, Danielle was the last passenger left on the bus, and the driver asked her where she was going. "I haven't a clue," she said, "I was hoping to find a Salvation Army hostel, but I'm not even sure there is one in this city."

"I know where the Salvation Army hostel is," said the bus driver. "I can drop you off right outside." And when he did, he even carried her bags into the hostel, where she stayed for the next three days free of charge, before they arranged for her to be taken back to the airport. God had blessed her with everything she needed so that she could abound in this good work.

"As it is written, 'He has scattered abroad his gifts to the poor; his righteousness endures forever." (2 Cor 9:9)

The scattering in this verse is not indiscriminate, as in the seed scattered in the parable of the sower. God has a definite focus, and his gifts in this case are meant for the poor. His righteousness endures forever, meaning he has not forgotten the poor, but does right by them. But his gifts don't appear to be getting there, because if they did, they wouldn't still be poor. So where have they gone? God wants to help the poor through the church, as happened very effectively in Acts 2 and 4, but more often than not we keep what we have been given to ourselves, instead of sharing what we have with the poor. We need to remember this when we think of each man giving what he has decided in his heart to give. Thinking back to 'takers and keepers', how much have we decided in our hearts to keep?

"Now he who supplies seed to the sower and bread for food will also supply and increase your store of seed and will enlarge the harvest of your righteousness." (2 Cor 9:10)

Just as the previous verse talked about God's righteousness enduring forever, here God looks to enlarge the harvest of our own righteousness. He wants us to do what is right by other people, just as God does. The words supply, increase and enlarge are part of the vocabulary of blessing, and we have a good example of God's blessing enabling us to bless others in the feeding of the five thousand in Matt 14:13-21.

The story begins with Jesus and his disciples withdrawing by boat to a solitary place to get some rest. But the crowds soon arrive, and Jesus has compassion on the crowd and spends all day healing their sick. (An example of Jesus considering the needs of others, rather than focussing on his own need to rest). As evening comes the disciples suggest that Jesus send the people away so they can go somewhere and buy food. Jesus has been demonstrating righteousness all day by ministering to the peoples' needs, and now it's the turn of the disciples to do what is right. Jesus says to his disciples, *"They do not need to go away. You give them something to eat."*

We all know what happens next. 'He who supplies seed to the sower' shows them that when they thought they had nothing to give, they did actually have five small loaves and two small fish. Actually they belonged to a young lad who offered up his food with open hands and an open heart, so that the hungry could be fed. The loaves were not as we normally think of them, but possibly the equivalent of five tuna sandwiches. Whatever the amount, it was pitiful when faced with a crowd of 5,000 men, plus women and children (Matt 5:21). The twelve disciples each had hundreds of people to feed.

It's important to note that Jesus did not feed the crowd. The disciples did. Jesus helped them to see that they did have something they could give, even though in their eyes it was pitifully small. Jesus prayed the blessing, and as they stepped out in obedience (which must have taken huge faith and courage, considering the pitiful amount they each had in their hands), God poured out his blessing, so much so that the food in their hands multiplied beyond belief, and they ended up picking up twelve basketfuls of leftovers. 'He who supplies bread for food' increased their supply and enlarged the harvest of their righteousness, all through the reward of blessing. They stepped out in faith and obedience, and God multiplied the blessing. One of the lessons for our giving is that we don't need to wait until we have plenty before we give to those in need. If we give what we have, God will somehow enable us to give all that is needed, and still have some left over for our own needs.

"You will be made rich in every way so that you can be generous on every occasion, and through us your generosity will result in thanksgiving to God." (2 Cor 9:11)

Notice the 'so that'. God is able to make all grace abound to you *so that* you will abound in every good work; you will be made rich in every way *so that* you can be generous on every occasion. God does not bless us with riches in order for us to hoard what we've been given and grow fat and wealthy. God gives to us *so that* we can give to others. When he sees that someone understands this principle, he will give them even more because he knows they will be generous and give what they've received to those who need it.

We can see this principle in the parable of the Talents in Matthew 25. The talent was a sum of money (approx. hundreds of pounds), and a master going on a long journey called his three servants to him and gave them a varying number of talents, *so that* they could invest the money, enabling the master to get a return on his capital while he was away. One servant was given five talents, the second was given two talents, and the third was given one talent. In the parable the master represents God, and the three servants represent the fact that different people have different amounts of money and wealth. Some more, some less. The point is though, that whether we have more or less, we have all received something from God that we can use to help others.

When the master returned home, he found that the first servant had invested his five talents and gained five more, and the master praised him. So too the second servant who had invested his two talents and gained two more. The third servant had not invested his one talent but hoarded it by burying it in the ground. The master was angry and rebuked him for not investing the money he had been entrusted with. He ordered that the one talent be taken from the third servant and given to the first servant, who by this time had accumulated ten talents. *"For everyone who has will be given more, and he will have an abundance. Whoever does not have, even what he has will be taken from him."* (Matt 25:29).

When people don't understand the principle it seems very unfair, but fairness has to be understood in the context of the poor and needy, whom God chooses to help by giving resources to his servants. He expects his servants (you and I) to pass on these resources to whoever needs them. No doubt there are many interpretations of this parable, but in this interpretation, investing the money represents giving it to those in need. The servant who buried his one talent was not being fair to those who could have benefited from that money. Sadly a lot of churches sit on money they've been given, rather than giving it away to provide for those in need. The first servant however, who was entrusted with a lot of money, 'invested' it where it was needed. The master knew he could be trusted to use the money according to his master's wishes, which is why he then received even more, as the more this servant received, the more needy people would benefit.

Paul ends this discussion on grace and blessing with thanksgiving.

"This service that you perform is not only supplying the needs of God's people but is also overflowing in many expressions of thanks to God. Because of the service by which you have proved yourselves, men will praise God for the obedience that accompanies your confession of the Gospel of Christ, and for your generosity in sharing with them and with everyone else. And in their prayers for you their hearts will go out to you, because of the surpassing grace God has given you." (2 Cor 9:12-14)

We do not give in order to be blessed. We give because God rules in our hearts, filling them with love and compassion, as we saw in the example of the Macedonian church. But our giving to others also overflows with thanksgiving. Zacchaeus gave generously to the poor as a way of saying 'Thank you' to Jesus who had accepted him and his friends with such love and grace. Those who receive help praise God, sometimes not knowing who has actually helped them, and when they do know their benefactor, their hearts go out to them in thankfulness. Imagine being the man who had been beaten up and robbed, in the story of the Good Samaritan. If that had been you or me, I imagine we would have felt indebted to the Good Samaritan for the rest of our lives. We would never forget him and would always thank God for him. I can think of many situations where a deep and lifelong friendship has become established between people who were once strangers to each other, simply because someone went the second mile to help a person in need.

"Thanks be to God for his indescribable gift!" (2 Cor 9:15)

Having warmed to his theme of the multiple blessings that come from generous giving, Paul turns his attention to the very source of generosity, and thanks God for the gift of his Son. An act of pure giving. Can anyone put into words what it meant for our Father to give his Son, knowing what mankind would do to him? Paul uses the word 'indescribable', but somehow we have to grasp what it meant for the Father to sacrifice or let go of his beloved Son. What does it really mean when we read those familiar words, *"God so love the world he gave his one and only son…"*? It is a tragedy that so many people see God as hard and unfeeling, allowing his Son to suffer and die on the Cross. Only a parent having to give up their child can begin to understand, and Penny experienced something close with the birth of our third child.

In 1985 our daughter, Becky, was born in Withybush Hospital, Haverfordwest. She was born a beautiful, healthy baby, and on the fourth day mother and baby arrived home. The next day however, Becky was not well and the doctor sent her straight back to the hospital for tests. Penny stayed with Becky at the hospital while I returned home for the inevitable milking. Cows have to be milked twice a day, come what may!

Late that Friday night Penny rang from the hospital. The tests had shown that Becky had bacterial meningitis. I was not familiar with meningitis at the time, and didn't realise at first the seriousness of the situation. The bacterial form can often be fatal in adults, and this was a five day old baby. During that night, as Penny stayed in a small side ward with our young baby, four different doctors were in and out of the ward doing what they could. Meningitis involves an inflammation of the fluids and membrane around the brain, causing a lot of pain, and as a result Becky would flinch at the slightest movement. The doctors put her on a concoction of strong drugs fed through a drip fastened to the side of her head.

As the night wore on there seemed little that the doctors could do to alleviate the pain. In between doctors and nurses going in and out, Penny prayed that God would heal our daughter and that everything would be fine. Time went by and there was no improvement, despite Penny's continued prayers. Eventually, in the early hours of the morning, Penny prayed simply that God would give her a sign, some sort of reassurance that everything would be alright, even if it was going to take some time.

What happened next was quite a shock, and an unpleasant one at that. As she prayed, Penny saw a clear picture of a tiny coffin, surrounded by pink flowers. The meaning seemed obvious, and Penny was shaken to her core. She redoubled the intensity of her prayers, pleading with Jesus to heal our baby. As she prayed she 'saw' Jesus in the corner of the room, holding out his hands, saying, "Give her to me." Because of the coffin, Penny assumed that Becky was going to die. Jesus seemed to be saying that she should give Becky to him and let her die. She knew Jesus could heal the sick and she prayed for healing.

The hours went by with no obvious change for better or worse. Every time she asked for healing she 'saw' Jesus, still with his hands open saying "Give her to me." After four hours of handing Becky over and then pulling her back at the last moment, Penny knew she had to let go.

This is not a story of having faith for healing. Penny honestly thought Becky was going to die. To let go at this stage was the greatest act of sacrifice any parent could be asked to make. The only crumb of comfort was a verse that came to her mind. "We know that in all things God works for the good of those who love him." (Ro 8:28). Perhaps, she thought, something good might come out of Becky's death.

Penny finally handed Becky over to Jesus in prayer, and left her in his hands. Immediately the temperamental drip settled down and the warning bleep went quiet. Becky went to sleep and slept soundly for the first time in 24 hours.

On Monday morning the chief paediatrician saw Becky for the first time, compared her notes with what he saw in front of him, and couldn't believe this was the same baby, as she was as bright as a button. The doctors who had been there insisted that the notes for Friday night were accurate, and that this was indeed the same baby. The paediatrician took her off two of the drugs, and three days later Penny asked for Becky to be discharged, as she had two other children at home. Reluctantly the doctors agreed, but said she would need to be brought back for checks once a week for the next few months. Three weeks later they accepted that she was showing no sign of any brain damage whatsoever, and she would no longer need monitoring on a weekly basis. Three months later, after our move to Cardiff in order for me to pursue theological training, the paediatrician at the Heath Hospital in Cardiff proclaimed that if anything, the meningitis seemed to have done her some good, as she was the brightest three month old baby that he'd seen for a long time!

Someone asked Penny why God had given her that picture of a tiny coffin if all along he intended to heal her? What Penny felt at the time was that God was saying, in effect, are you willing to give me your baby even if it means she might die? Penny was asked to give up her baby. Abraham was asked to give up his son. In the event, both lived, but when God gave up his own Son, he knew without a shadow of doubt that his Son would suffer and die, in order that you and I might receive forgiveness and eternal life. The blessing of the Resurrection on Easter Day came as the result of a pure act of giving on God's part.

"Thanks be to God for his indescribable gift".

PART 5

PUTTING TEACHING
INTO PRACTICE

13 Should Christians Tithe?

I t's one thing to learn what the Bible teaches; it's another thing to put it into practice. Jesus said that everyone who heard his teaching and put it into practice is like a wise man who built his house on the rock (Matt 7:24). In order to do that he had to dig down into the rock to lay a foundation. It was hard work, and it was tempting to find somewhere easier and build a house on sand, but in the end it was worth the effort.

We need to be realistic. Christians who exhibit a new attitude marked with compassion and generosity are to be admired. But not all of us can claim to be like Zacchaeus or the early church on the Day of Pentecost. To be honest, a lot of us are more like Ananias and Sapphira, in that we do give, but more often than not we keep back a lot for ourselves. The level of generosity, and our attitude towards giving, varies tremendously across the Christian Church, of all denominations and none. In some churches the giving is exceedingly generous, in others it is abysmal. In 2016 the Evangelical Alliance stated that *"statistics suggest that most Christians give away two per cent or less of their income, with a small percentage of Christians never giving at all."*[18]

What holds many of us back is our fear that if we give away too much, then we ourselves will be left wanting. We want soft hearts

---

18   Caroline Gregory, *'Black Friday or Giving Tuesday?'* Evangelical Alliance
       Nov 24th 2016

filled with compassion, but we either don't sense the divine prompting as we should, or we haven't yet learned to trust God as the great provider. Like my experience at Spring Harvest all those years ago, we want to give generously but we can't help thinking of the bills that need paying. Despite the fact that we receive a new heart when we come to Christ, we are still surrounded by the habits of others, within the church as well as out. The early Christians were surrounded by three thousand others of like mind and heart, but most of us don't have that advantage. For good or ill, we are more affected than we realise by the habits and attitudes of those around us. So where do we go from here? And where do we start?

This is where we need to grasp the nettle of tithing. For many Christians, the problem is that we hear two viewpoints, each put forward with equal enthusiasm. Some say that the command to tithe still applies to Christians, with the assertion in Malachi 3 that if we do not tithe then we are robbing God. Others insist, equally forcibly, that tithing is part of the Old Testament Law which no longer applies to Christians who live under grace, not law. The abuse of tithing over the centuries is also put forward as another good reason to avoid tithing.

In mediaeval and Victorian times, people were forced by the church authorities to tithe their crops into tithe barns overflowing with plenty, which then went to enrich an established church which had little concern for those living in poverty. In more recent times there have been many horror stories of church leaders putting pressure on people to tithe, and in some cases the tithe seems to benefit the church and its leaders more than the poor. Stuart Murray gives a comprehensive coverage of the abuse of tithing through the ages, in his book 'Beyond Tithing'.

His conclusion is that *'Tithing is biblical, but not Christian.'* [19]
There is enough evidence of the abuse of tithing to put some
people off for life, but we need to remember the wise words of
a well-respected Christian leader, David Watson. When talking
about the abuse of spiritual gifts, he said, *'the answer to abuse is
not disuse, but right use.'* This same wisdom applies equally to the
abuse of tithing.

On a more positive note, there are many respected theologians and
others who firmly believe that tithing should be very much part
and parcel of the Christian life. R.T.Kendall, in his book 'The Gift
of Giving', endorsed by George Carey, Billy Graham, John Stott
and others, has this to say about the Christian practice of tithing.
*"Apart from the fact that were all Christians to tithe it would solve
the Church's financial problems, I am sure that becoming a tither
provides a definite breakthrough for every Christian. It unlocks the
door of his heart, mind and will. It releases. It emancipates. It frees.
Becoming a tither is a milestone in a Christian's life."* [20]

The Evangelical Alliance had this to say about tithing in the
context of Christian giving. *"The sad fact is this: where the doctrine
of tithing has been thrown out, often so has generous giving
altogether. Conveniently, no compulsion to tithe has resulted in
Christians adopting a far lazier approach to giving. Undisciplined
as we generally are, yet again we seem to prove that we don't do
well when given freedom to respond to general principles, and that
rules are sometimes for our benefit. If we can't be trusted to adopt
the radical giving modelled in the New Testament, a requirement to
tithe might be a good starting point."* [21]

19   Stuart Murray, *'Beyond Tithing'*. Paternoster Press 2000. P.88

20   R.T.Kendall, *'The Gift of Giving'* Hodder and Stoughton 1998 P.15

21   Caroline Gregory, *'Black Friday or Giving Tuesday?'* Article for Evangelical
      Alliance 24th Nov 2016

I became convinced of the value of tithing, not through the preaching of some passionate advocate, but through my own examination of tithing in the context of the overall teaching on giving in the Bible, in both the Old and New Testaments. The evidence in the Old Testament is clear and has already been presented. The key question for Christians, and the more difficult one to answer, concerns what evidence we find in the New Testament for the continued practice of tithing.

For the sake of clarity I shall ask three simple questions about tithing, and then reflect on them in the light of the Bible's teaching and my own experience of tithing, both individually and in the church, over the last thirty years. What did Jesus teach? What did the apostles teach? What was the practice of the early church?

WHAT DID JESUS TEACH?

When we turn to Matthew, the teaching of Jesus begins in earnest in chapter five, commonly referred to as the Sermon on the Mount. Straightaway Jesus makes a very interesting comment on the relationship between his own teaching and that of the Old Testament. "*Do not think that I have come to abolish the Law or the Prophets; I have not come to abolish them but to fulfil them. I tell you the truth, until heaven and earth disappear, not the smallest letter, nor the least stroke of a pen, will by any means disappear from the Law until everything is accomplished.*" (Matt 5:17,18)

Having declared his intention not to abolish the Law, he then shows very clearly what he means by 'fulfilling the Law'. In the verses that follow, Jesus takes one Old Testament law after another and goes far beyond the letter of the law to the very heart or spirit of the law. So for instance,

'*Do not murder your brother*' becomes '*Do not be angry with your brother*'.

'*Do not commit adultery*' becomes '*Do not look at anyone with lust in your heart*'.

'Do not divorce except with a certificate' becomes *'Do not divorce at all, except for marital unfaithfulness'.*

'Do not break an oath that you have sworn to the Lord' becomes *'Do not swear any oaths. Simply let your 'yes' be 'yes' and your 'no' be 'no'.*

'An eye for an eye, and a tooth for a tooth' becomes *'Turn the other cheek'.*

'Love your neighbour and hate your enemy' becomes *'Love your enemy and pray for those who persecute you'.*

In everything he says, Jesus makes the Law more radical. Extremely radical. He does not deal specifically with tithing so we have to ask, 'How do you make tithing more radical?' He never mentions ten per cent, but on three occasions he implies one hundred per cent. He commends a poor widow who gave everything she had left, and challenges first the rich young man and then the disciples to sell all their possessions and give to the poor. On another occasion Mary anoints his feet with perfume so expensive it was worth a year's wages, and again he commends her.

Tithing itself is only mentioned twice in the Gospels, in Lk 11:42 and Lk 18:13, though Luke 11 is also repeated in Matt 23:23. On both these occasions Jesus berates the Pharisees for their arrogant and hypocritical attitude. It is worth noting the comment at the end of Luke 11 v42. *"Woe to you Pharisees, because you give God a tenth of your mint, rue and all other kinds of garden herbs, but you neglect justice and the love of God. You should have practiced the latter, without leaving the former undone."* In the Living Bible, Kenneth Taylor paraphrases this verse by saying, *'You should tithe, yes, but you should not leave these other things undone."* It is clear that Jesus is not decrying the practice of tithing, but the hypocritical way in which it was practiced.

These are the only occasions where Jesus specifically mentions tithing. There is however, another passage which many would see as having specific relevance to tithing. Matthew records an occasion when the Pharisees asked Jesus if Jews should pay taxes to Caesar. The question was meant as a trap. If Jesus answered no, he would be in trouble with the Romans; on the other hand an affirmative answer would not be popular with the Jews, who deeply resented having to pay taxes to the Romans. Jesus' answer astonished them. Calling for a roman coin, he asked whose portrait was inscribed on it. *"Caesar's.' they replied. Then he said to them, 'Give to Caesar what is Caesar's, and to God what is God's."* (Matt 22:21).

The Jews would certainly have understood that he was telling them to ensure they gave the tithe to God, as well as paying the Roman tax. The essence of Jesus' answer is simple and clear. Don't cheat the tax man, and don't try to cheat God.

Let's also consider how Jesus spoke about the Sabbath. The Sabbath was another of God's laws which was being meticulously observed by the Jewish leaders, but in such a legalistic way that Jesus rebuked them fiercely. Again they focussed on unimportant detail, but overlooked justice and mercy. They complained that Jesus' disciples were picking grains of corn to eat as they walked through a corn field on the Sabbath, and then were horrified when Jesus healed a man with a crippled hand on the Sabbath. Jesus only said one positive thing about the Sabbath, and that was his comment that the Sabbath was made for man, not man for the Sabbath (Mark 2:27). Nearly every other comment about the Sabbath is in the context of his berating the Jewish leaders for their legalistic attitude and their lack of compassion. But does that mean that Jesus wanted them to stop observing the Sabbath? Absolutely not. He wanted them to continue observing the Sabbath, but in a way more honouring to God and which showed grace and mercy to others. The early church chose to observe the Sabbath on a Sunday rather than a Saturday, but the principle is still observed.

The same is true of many other commands and spiritual disciplines found in the Old Testament. The practices of tithing, of keeping the Sabbath, of prayer and of fasting, all have one thing in common. They are all practices commanded in the Old Testament, for which the Pharisees were rebuked in the New Testament. Not because there is anything wrong with tithing, keeping the Sabbath, praying or fasting. Far from it. The problem was the hypocrisy and cold hearted legalism with which the Pharisees practised their religion, as Jesus makes clear in Matt 6:1-18. Having rebuked the Pharisees for their hypocrisy, Jesus makes it very clear that he still wants his hearers to practice these things, but with humility. So he says, in effect, when you give, pray and fast, do not do it the way the Pharisees do; do it this way. I believe that Jesus would say, when you tithe don't do it that way; do it this way.

We need to remember that Jesus and the apostles, and for that matter the bulk of the people whom Jesus taught, were all practising Jews before they became Christians, and as such they would have been brought up to tithe. This is equally true of the majority of Christians in the early years of the church. So if the majority of the early Christians had been brought up to tithe, and assuming for a moment that Jesus wanted them to stop tithing, then surely he would have to spell it out to them clearly? The very fact that he hardly ever mentions tithing seems clear proof that he didn't want them to stop tithing. That sounds contradictory, but to say nothing in the context of an established practice is to encourage the status quo. He taught instead that they should expand their giving in a very radical way. Tithing was not abolished but fulfilled. The key question is how it was fulfilled.

WHAT DID THE APOSTLES TEACH?

After the Gospels, tithing is never mentioned as such in the New Testament, except in Hebrews where tithing is only mentioned in the context of an historical discussion on Melchizedek. However,

Paul states clearly in 1 Cor 16:2 that each one should set aside a sum of money in proportion to their income, on a regular basis, every Sunday. Putting this alongside Jesus' clear intent on making the law more radical, can only mean that Paul meant that they should give more than ten per cent, but like Jesus he was unwilling to name an upper limit. Instead he encouraged them all to *'excel in this grace of giving'*. Furthermore, Paul says very clearly that each person should be free to give what they want to give, *"not reluctantly or under compulsion, for God loves a cheerful giver."* (2 Cor 9:7). Putting these teachings together, Paul seems to be implying that our giving in proportion to our income should be greater than ten per cent, but given freely from the heart.

Paul, James and John all have strong things to say about the rich who refuse to share with the poor, and Paul in particular warns against the love of money being a root of all kinds of evil (2 Tim 6:10). Both of these areas are addressed through tithing, as we saw in the previous chapter.

WHAT WAS THE PRACTICE OF THE EARLY CHURCH?

The record of Acts 2 and 4 makes it clear that the early church took the teaching of Jesus on giving, radical though it was, absolutely seriously. Selling land and houses, they gave to the poor and had everything in common. This is so far removed from tithing as to make it virtually redundant. I would however, make one comment in connection with tithing. The sheer extent of this generous giving has rarely been repeated throughout the history of the church. In fact quite the opposite. Today, most Christians struggle to give more than two per cent. Could it be that the early church actually had a head start because they were already used to tithing? Yes, they were filled with the Holy Spirit, fuelled by the teaching of Jesus and encouraged by the enthusiasm of thousands of other likeminded people around them, but would their giving have been the same if they weren't already accustomed to the principles of worship, sacrifice, obedience, faith and blessing in regard to their giving? No-one today can answer that question with authority, but the thought behind the question has real value. To quote a modern day phrase, 'You can't run before you can walk.' To what extent can we give with an open hand if we haven't yet learned to open the clenched fist?

In his second letter to the Corinthians, Paul highlights the example of the Macedonian church and their generous donation, against the background of their own poverty and persecution. In 2 Cor 8:5 he says, "*And they did not do as we expected, but they gave themselves first to the Lord and then to us in keeping with God's will.*" My own understanding of this verse is that the Macedonians first gave a tithe or 'tithe equivalent' (which could have been more than ten per cent) to their own poor, who Paul has already stated were in 'extreme poverty', and then on top of that gave a generous donation to the poor in Judea. An action which Paul describes as being '*in keeping with God's will*'. Giving '*first to the Lord*' would be a natural way of describing the tithe, which belonged to the Lord and was holy to the Lord. '*In keeping with God's will*' would also be a natural way of referring to the practice of tithing. The fact that this offering was given from the heart chimes perfectly with Paul's insistence that each man should give what he has decided in his heart to give. There is no reason at all why a tithe can't be given from the heart.

Personally I find it hard to see how else this verse can be interpreted. I've read the suggestion that giving themselves first to the Lord was an indication of their spiritual commitment; that they 'gave themselves first to Christ,' and the Lord told them to give generously, but that doesn't make sense in the context of the passage. It would imply that asking the Lord in this way was not something that Paul expected: '*they did not do as we expected, but they gave themselves first to the Lord.*' Highly unlikely, I would have thought, considering his description of this very spiritual church overflowing with joy despite their difficult circumstances.

The fact is that their response did take him by surprise, because they chose to give their normal tithe to their own poor, and on top of that gave generously to the poor in Judea.

Some will argue that the Macedonians were Gentiles and therefore wouldn't have known tithing, but it's not as simple as that. The Macedonian churches were based mainly in Philippi, Thessalonica, and Berea. Although there is no record of a synagogue in Philippi, Paul preached at the synagogues in both Thessalonica and Berea, and many of the Jews believed and became the nucleus of the new church. The new Jewish believers in Berea are described as being, *"of more noble character than the Thessalonians, for they received the message with great eagerness and examined the Scriptures every day to see if what Paul said was true. Many of the Jews believed..."* (Acts 17:11)

This description of the believers in Berea, being of noble character and receiving the Gospel with great eagerness, echoes the ethos of the Macedonian church in 2 Corinthians 8. The fact that they held the Old Testament scriptures in such high regard implies that they would have been confirmed tithers before they became Christians.

CONCLUSION

If we are to journey towards Christian giving, then tithing is a great place to start. What I like about tithing is that it helps us develop good habits; not just good habits about giving sacrificially on a regular basis, but also good habits in the way we think about God and about the poor. I love the Living Bible translation of Dt 14:23, *"The purpose of tithing is to teach you always to put God first in your lives."* It certainly did that for me. And what's more it helped me to prioritise the poor and needy a lot more than I had done previously. It also helped me to enjoy giving. Occasionally we would receive a significant gift or payment, and once we had started tithing, this gift or payment was always followed with the same question. "Who are we going to give the tithe to?" Having money that had to be given away was a new experience, and when it became a regular one, it was not only exciting but exhilarating. Giving became enjoyable and truly fulfilling.

In my experience, the key to Christian tithing is the ability to do so without being legalistic. This means holding lightly to the questions of detail, such as tithing before or after tax, and so on. There is good scriptural reason for giving the tithe to the local church, but again that is a principle not a prescription. I find it freeing to hold together the command to tithe with Paul's exhortation that *"Each man should give what he has decided in his heart to give."* At Broad Haven I had taught on tithing, on and off, for four years before I suggested the church should tithe the church income. It took that long before the majority of church members felt comfortable to do this. Even then, and for the rest of my time at Broad Haven, individual members were always encouraged to give what they felt was right to give. It was the positive testimony of other people who had chosen to tithe, and who testified enthusiastically about their experience, that gradually led to more and more people choosing to tithe themselves.

If the principle of tithing is going to be fulfilled as opposed to abolished, part of that fulfilment is that tithing should come from the heart. We tithe not because we have to but because we want to; because we have decided this is going to be part of our giving. For this reason, I don't believe that pressure to tithe from the pulpit is appropriate. Teaching yes, but not pressure overladen with guilt.

There are many good and practical reasons for Christians to tithe, most of which have already been covered. The important question for all Christians is to ask, "Will tithing help me to move towards the level and quality of Christian giving that Jesus taught and Paul encouraged when he said, *'See that you also excel in this grace of giving?'*

Personally I take the view that the practice of tithing is a very helpful step on the journey towards a deeper level of rich generosity. Think of tithing as a diving board. When I lived by the sea at Broad Haven there were times when the sea was very cold. Would-be swimmers would dip their toes in the water and hastily retreat, whereas others would wade in slowly, taking time to adjust to the cold temperature. Many only went so far and then withdrew, leaving the bravest of the brave to dive in and start swimming. A diving board takes away that process of 'shall I, shan't I?' You literally dive straight in, and you're already swimming before you have time to think about the temperature. I like to think of tithing as a spiritual diving board which helps us to dive straight in to the river of grace which is the New Testament experience of generous giving.

Another picture is the ministry of John the Baptist. God in his wisdom decided the Jewish people needed the ministry of John before they were ready for Jesus. John prepared the way for the one who would come after him, and when Jesus appeared, John stepped back. Having gone ahead and prepared the way he said, 'He must become greater; I must become less.' (John 3:30)

I think of tithing as preparing us to 'excel in this grace of giving'. We are not meant to stop at tithing; we should go further, just as John's disciples needed to go further and follow Christ. When Christ appeared, John stepped back and made himself less. There was a time when I used to think of tithing as the last word on Christian giving, but now I'm stepping back. I still tithe, but I'm learning to give on top of my tithing as and when I see the need. As we go deeper into grace we find a lesser emphasis on tithing and a greater emphasis on giving generously from the heart, above and beyond tithing.

Think of rich generosity as a spacecraft, and tithing as the rocket used to blast the spacecraft into space. A spacecraft can't get into space on its own, because of the restraining pull of gravity keeping it within the earth's atmosphere. The rocket is needed for that initial blast to take the spacecraft through and beyond the atmosphere. Once the spacecraft clears the atmosphere, the rocket can be jettisoned as it is no longer needed.

Most of us struggle to give generously because it's a concept so alien to the general atmosphere around us, both within and outside the church. We can't help being affected by that psychological gravity in society which pulls us back, and it's so strong it's really hard to break out from the world's way of thinking. The world says 'look after number one', and if we get beyond that way of thinking, we're still influenced by the regular airline advice, which is to attach your own air mask before you attempt to attach your child's mask, because you have to look after yourself first if you're going to be effective in looking after others. That may be appropriate on an aeroplane, but not for Christian giving.

Those who don't agree with tithing may have noticed that I've just suggested it can be jettisoned at some point as it is no longer needed. I agree. But how many of us have reached that point where we've broken completely clear of the pull of the world's view on money, wealth and giving? Let me tell you my own story of how tithing became my diving board, and the rocket that took me beyond the gravitational pull of looking after number one.

Some years after my tithing was all neat and sorted, or so I thought, the Lord took me a step further. Soon after we arrived at Broad Haven, a minister friend of mine had a problem with his car. It turned out to be beyond repair, and he needed another car rather urgently, but had very little available money with which to pay for it. He couldn't buy just any car as his wife required an automatic. It so happened that at the same time I knew of a car for sale in Broad Haven. One of those classic 'low mileage, good condition, one careful lady owner' cars, and an automatic to boot!

Then came one of those promptings. I really felt God was telling me to get this car for my friend. It was extremely good value, but at a cost of £2,000 it was more than he could afford. I decided God must be prompting me to pray the money in. Consequently I did just that. I gave it all to God in prayer. He knew my friend's need. He knew as well as I did that this car was exceptionally good value, and that it was the perfect car for my friend and his wife. They had managed with old wrecks for some years but now they had a young family, they really needed something more reliable. The Bible says, *"Ask and it shall be given you."* I felt emboldened to do just that, and prayed that somehow the money would be provided.

Two days later a cheque for £1,000 arrived in the post, as a gift. I mentioned in an earlier chapter about a similar cheque which came my way following the death of an elderly Aunt in New Zealand. I don't make a habit of receiving £1,000 cheques, and it has only happened twice in my entire life. Anyway, there I was only two days after praying, with a cheque for £1,000 in my hand! Penny agreed that this money should be put towards the car, and suitably encouraged, I began praying for the rest of the money. I said earlier that seeing the blessing of God as he provides, has a wonderful effect on your faith. That was certainly true in this case, and my prayers became so full of faith that to coin a phrase, the money was already in the bank. Only now, God seemed to change tack and started playing the "last minute" game. After only two days wait for the first cheque, the next one took a lot longer. After two weeks had gone by the 'one careful lady owner' was asking if I still wanted the car. She was buying a new one and didn't want two cars in her drive. The new car was arriving the following week.

I prayed more earnestly, but nothing happened. Well, that's not entirely accurate. As I prayed, I felt God saying something to me which I didn't really want to hear. I felt he was saying, "Ifor, I've given you a thousand pounds. Why don't you give the other thousand?" It would have been convenient to be able to say I didn't have the money but that wasn't true. I was still in the process of waiting for the promised house to come available, and I had funds in a savings account from before our time in college. I tried to tell God I needed the money for the house, but he didn't seem to be listening. The 'one careful lady owner' was getting a bit agitated as the days went by, and it wasn't fair to keep an old lady waiting. We had to make a decision. Penny and I prayed and the decision was made. We took a thousand pounds out of the account, bought the car, and delivered it to our friends, who were absolutely delighted. It was far beyond tithing, but God had brought me to a diving board, and from there I had plunged straight in to the river of grace.

I firmly believe the ideal of Christian giving is to give generously and willingly from the heart, both on a regular basis and also spontaneously, as the need arises. I also firmly believe that one of the best ways to reach that position is to grasp the nettle and start tithing; not because you must, but because you can; because when you do, you learn to be generous.

14 A Local Church Learns to be Generous

This is the story of a church that learned to tithe, and then to give generously. A church that grew in faith and love, as well as numbers. The one led to the other. When I was first introduced to Broad Haven Baptist Church, I was a young minister fresh out of theological college, and they were a traditional rural Baptist church in the small seaside village of Broad Haven in Pembrokeshire, a delightful holiday area with a population of less than a thousand people.

In 1988, the church was one of a group of three small churches which had formerly shared a minister, but now for reasons beyond their control they faced the prospect of having to call and finance a minister on their own. The 22 members at the church meeting were faced with a stark choice. If they wanted to call a minister they would have to double the offering, even with the Baptist Union providing a grant to pay half the minister's stipend. It was one of those occasions which brings to mind the old story about the church treasurer who addressed the church meeting with good news and bad news. "The good news," he said, "is that we have all the money we need to pay the bills and the minister's stipend. The bad news is that it's still in your pockets!"

It's one thing to joke about such things. It's quite another to recognise the truth and to respond in faith. Yes, we've got the money in our pockets or bank accounts, but how willing are we to let go and give? That night the church made a decision which

I believe the Lord has been honouring ever since. They pledged themselves to double the offering and call me as their minister. I arrived with Penny and four children in July of that same year. The children were a big boost to the Sunday School, and even more so when our fifth child was born the following year.

The previous year's accounts showed an offering of £4,500. True to their word the church doubled their giving, and the offering the following year increased to £9,000. As the church learned to let go and give, we gradually weaned ourselves off the Baptist Union grant, and 17 years later the church was having two morning services every Sunday and employing two ordained ministers, both on a full stipend completely financed by the church.

The decision to call a second minister was made at another church meeting in 2004, where again a clear choice had to be made. Most churches with just over 100 members wouldn't see the need for two ministers, but we felt there was so much more we could do in the community with an extra minister, and we decided to go for it. Not because we could easily afford two ministers, but because the church was still learning to let go and give, as well as putting the needs of others first and trusting God to meet our own needs.

After outlining the vision of what we felt could be achieved with an extra minister focussing on youth and young families in the area, we came down to brass tacks and talked about money. The church was already giving generously but in order to finance a second full time minister the offering would have to increase by another thirty per cent. The decision was the same; to let go and give. In 2005 we called a young married minister fresh out of college, and for the following three years the church dug deep in their pockets and funded two full time ministers. When the assistant minister moved on after his three year probationary period, the church decided not to call another second minister, not because we couldn't afford it but because it was felt we needed to focus more on developing and utilising the gifts of the members themselves.

PRAYER

As is so often the case, this story begins with prayer. In my last month at Broad Haven I had a conversation with a holidaymaker who had not visited the church for 29 years. He recalled a dark and dismal chapel with a small congregation, one of whom invited him to join them at their Monday evening prayer meeting. There were two, sometimes three, old ladies who met every Monday to pray that God would do a new thing in Broad Haven. Thank God for old ladies who pray! Where would the church be without them? If anyone reading this book is asking where to start, there's your answer. You don't have to be an old lady, but you do need to pray, preferably with someone else.

The prayers of these elderly ladies at Broad Haven began to be answered through the ministry of my predecessor, David Waters. Despite having to look after three chapels he invested a lot of time and effort into the young peoples' work at Broad Haven, and I was able to reap the harvest when we baptised 7 teenagers and two adults in my first year. I am convinced it was the faithful prayers of these prayer warriors that led to the momentous decision to double the offering in 1988, but that was only the beginning. Little did they know what they'd let themselves in for! For that matter, neither did I.

THE CHALLENGE TO TITHE

My first month at Broad Haven was interesting, to say the least, especially where the preaching was concerned. On the day before my induction, with a sermon series already planned for the first month, God spoke to me very forcibly through my daily readings, and caused me to ditch what I'd planned and prepared, and preach instead on the consequences of adultery! It was not something I would have chosen for my first sermon in a new church, but I was reading through 2 Samuel 11 at the time, and the story of David committing adultery with Bathsheba just leapt out from the page. To make matters worse, the following week I found myself in 2 Samuel 13, where David's son Amnon commits incest with his half-sister Tamar. Yes, you've guessed it, the story leapt out from the page and I found myself preaching on the taboo subject of incest. The poor congregation were probably thinking they'd made a big mistake. I well remember one of them shaking my hand at the door and saying, "Well, I can't wait for next week!"

I could never work out why I had to preach on such topics in my first two weeks, but now, looking back with hindsight, I think the Lord set me up. He was simply testing me to see if I'd be willing to preach what he wanted me to preach, whatever that might be. In other words, he was teaching me to be obedient. At the end of the first month I felt led to preach on tithing. I wouldn't have planned to preach on the topic at such an early stage, but as I say, I think the Lord set me up.

Sunday came and I began preaching on tithing. I could see from people's reaction that for many of the congregation this was not familiar teaching. As I came to the end of my sermon, I asked the treasurer to come to the pulpit. He did so rather hesitantly, not knowing what to expect. (In those early weeks, no-one knew what to expect!) With the treasurer in front of me I produced my first pay cheque, and read out the amount. Then I produced a second cheque of my own, written out to the church for a tenth of my month's pay, and handed it over to the treasurer. I then announced that although I would not be making a habit of doing this in public, from then on I would ensure that a tenth of my stipend was given back to the church. I merely wanted to show that I would be practising what I preached, and that I did not expect anyone to do anything I wasn't first prepared to do myself.

I didn't rush things, and it was not until four years later that the Church Meeting, at my suggestion, agreed to tithe the church offering. Individuals were free to give what they wanted to give, with no compulsion or pressure at all, but I felt the church as a body should take a lead and tithe the offering in order to give ten per cent to God's work outside the church. At the time I challenged the church to try it for 12 months, quoting Malachi 3, where God invites us to test him in the matter of tithing, promising to pour out his blessing in response.

The decision was made hesitantly at first, but then as faith and understanding grew, the church became more confident. I firmly believe that the church's decision to tithe, and the blessing that followed, was a key factor in the spiritual and numerical growth that has since occurred. God had brought together a church that had the faith to double its offering, with a minister who was now challenging them not only to dig deep, but to start giving it away. In God's economy that's a powerful combination, but not without its challenges.

When I first suggested the church start tithing, I was met with a phrase I was to hear time and time again. "Charity begins at home!" (Which sometimes means it stays at home as well). What they meant was that the church had an obligation to pay the minister, as well as the other regular bills, and it would be dishonest to start giving money away if we didn't have enough to meet our responsibilities. The principle sounds absolutely fine, until you start thinking of scriptural principles. As Christians are we going to attempt our various responsibilities in our own strength, or are we going to put God first and do it his way? Bearing in mind that if we do it our own way, we will invariably be looking after our own needs and not helping anyone else. At the end of the day we are faced with a choice. Our way or God's way? Our needs or the needs of others? Jesus' answer is simple and to the point. *"Seek first his kingdom and his righteousness, and all these things will be given to you as well."* (Matt 6:33).

As the church tithed its offering, they began to see the Lord provide, and their faith began to grow. It wasn't easy, and at times it was scary. A year or so later we had our first Gift Day. In the past they had raised money through jumble sales, though that had stopped before I arrived. Incredibly the Gift Day raised well over £3,000, an unheard of amount in those days. I was encouraged, and so were many others. As people tentatively began to give more, they were encouraged by the clear evidence around them that others were giving more as well.

A new attitude was developing, and the offering continued to rise as more and more people decided to tithe. What made a real difference were the "faith stories" that people began to hear, including the miraculous provision of our house. The difference soon became evident in our Deacons meetings. On one memorable occasion, not only did one deacon suggest we needed some drums to augment the music on Sunday mornings, but another deacon suggested we buy some drums with money from the church account! That may not seem remarkable to some churches, but for us that was a sure sign of a huge change in attitude.

When other Christian organisations or missionary groups sent appeals for money, the deacons were often outbidding each other on how much to give. In fact they were usually outbid by the treasurer, who was more sold on tithing than anybody. She could see the results first hand! As the annual offering increased year by year, more and more of the older members could be heard saying how much better this was than the old days, when they would work hard preparing a jumble sale, and have very little to show for it afterwards. A real change of attitude was taking place.

FOCUS ON OTHER CHURCHES

One of the blessings of tithing is that you always have money to give away. This meant we were constantly being led to focus on other situations outside our own church which deserved our support. One of those situations was a struggling Baptist church in nearby Neyland. At one time Neyland was a thriving town with a bustling port and a railway station, at the very end of the Great Western Railway. Over the years Milford Haven became the major port in the area, and the railway station at Neyland had closed. This meant that Neyland had become literally a "dead end" town. It was not on a through route, and no one went there unless they lived there. An example of the general air of malaise was that all four nonconformist chapels now had tiny congregations, and there hadn't been a full time nonconformist minister in the town for 35 years.

Such was the situation when the church at Broad Haven encouraged me to become moderator of Bethesda Baptist, Neyland. The role involved me taking the communion service once a month, and offering some leadership to the struggling congregation. The chapel building was in a terrible state, and the small single figure congregation met in the vestry for Sunday service. There were some new houses being built in Neyland, and the population of the town was approximately 4,500.

Over a period of time the Lord showed us he wanted to do a new thing in Neyland, and with the help of the Association and Union as well as many other sources, we were able to raise enough funds to call a minister/evangelist. Steve Lee was called in 2000 and the Lord blessed the work. The regular Sunday congregation grew to over 70 people, and the buildings were greatly improved, including the addition of a new kitchen, toilets and café area to help the church reach out into the community. What impressed me about the congregation at Broad Haven was their willingness to commit £2,000 a year for five years to support the new minister's stipend.

The focus on other churches widened as more and more of our members started preaching and taking services in local chapels, some of them offering to provide musical support as well as preaching.

COMMUNITY FOCUS

On one occasion a visiting minister was so impressed with what he saw God doing in Broad Haven that he encouraged his large city church to send a donation to encourage us in the work. A cheque for £1,000 was duly received. At the time the local community was trying to raise money for a skate park for the village youngsters, and the church meeting voted to put this unexpected cheque towards the local fund for the skate park. This was not a lack of gratitude, rather the expression of a new attitude that we should be giving to the needs of others rather than focussing on our own needs.

This new attitude extended towards the Village Hall. The hall is situated alongside the chapel and because of an ancient covenant the church had free use of the hall on Sundays. The Village Hall desperately needed new toilets but didn't have money to pay for them. The chapel also needed toilets, in fact they had been waiting for over 150 years, but we had no space to put them anywhere. On one memorable occasion during a Harvest Supper we had a line of ladies in our house across the road, queuing up to use the bathroom.

It was suggested at a church meeting that we co-operate with the Village Hall and build a new toilet block on our land as an extension to the hall. The extension would be paid for by the church, but with the provision of inner and outer doors the toilets could be used at any time by both groups. Another generous Gift Day produced a total of £11,000 from church members, and the rest of the sum needed was made up from grants obtained by the church. The church benefited from an extra room which was built over the extension, and the Village Hall and local community were very pleased to have some up to date toilet and shower facilities, at a nominal rent of £1 per year.

One night the Deacons meeting received a letter from the local community council. For many years the council had supported the four local churches by paying an annual grant of approximately

£130 each to help with the upkeep of the graveyards. After many years of giving such grants to local groups, they were aware that needs had changed in some areas, and there were other situations to which they wanted to grant aid. Accordingly they sent a letter to all local recipients, asking whether the grant was still needed. After consideration by the deacons, it was recognised that we no longer needed the money as we once did, and the treasurer was asked to write accordingly and thank them for their kind support over the years. The reply we received from the clerk to the Community Council is one of my favourite letters. I have it on file in the office, and it's the sort of letter you get out and read when you're having a bad day and need some encouragement. The letter was addressed to our treasurer, Glenys, and I have reproduced it in full.

Dear Glenys,

Thank you for your letter you passed to me before last night's meeting. I read it out and there was a spontaneous appreciation of the generous content (apparently they all clapped!). *Members asked me to write to you to express their admiration of not only the letter but of the whole organisation of your successful church and its truly Christian attitude. I know I speak for every member when I say that we hope your church (and its finances!) goes from strength to strength but if your circumstances do change the Havens Community Council will listen sympathetically to any requests you make.*

This letter highlights an important lesson. The church's attitude to money has a significant impact on the community, for good or ill. If the church is taking rather than giving, our so called Christian witness can have a hugely damaging effect. How many people, when someone from the local church knocks on their door, automatically assume the church wants their money? The good favour we began to receive from the community was part of God's promised blessing, as we continued to let go and give. One of the blessings was when we learned to work with the community, and not just for the community.

WILLING VOLUNTEERS

Sometime previously the Baptist church in nearby Johnston had been given the opportunity to use an empty shop for charity, raising funds for various needs in the Developing World. It started well, but after a while there just weren't enough volunteers to staff the shop on a regular basis, and it looked as if it would have to close. Our church secretary, Francis Maull, was related to one of the volunteers and brought the matter to our attention. We decided to take it on, and Francis enlisted the help of our own members to work alongside the original volunteers from Johnston. It was a fairly normal charity shop where people would donate used clothing, books and bric a brac, which were then sold very cheaply.

The volunteers were mainly elderly or retired people from both churches, who saw an opportunity to give their time so that needy people could be blessed. There are all sorts of ways of giving, and for many older people in the church, this was a way in which they could make a real difference. Neither church received any funds from the charity shop, and once a quarter the volunteers would sit down together and decide which charities would benefit. This gave an added bonus as each volunteer felt more personally involved with the people who were being helped. They amazing thing about this local project sustained by a group of pensioners, is that in just nine years, £150,000 has been given to needy people. Now in their tenth year, they are hoping to reach a new target of £25,000 given away in one year.

MISSION FOCUS

By now we had weaned ourselves off the grant from the Baptist Union and were self-supporting. However, although we were getting more involved in our local community, our involvement in overseas mission was not great, to say the least. An opportunity came when we heard of a project in Romania which involved building a school and medical centre for a Roma community. We intended to send groups out to help with the building, and also to work in the community, particularly among the children. It was the first time as a church that we had been so actively involved in overseas mission. We were the only outside group connected with the project and it needed a lot of finance. After a long discussion in the church meeting we agreed to kick start the project by donating £5,000 from church funds. It was a big decision, but again we saw the need to let go and help others.

That particular incident had an interesting sequel. A week later I was taking a funeral for a local man whose family all lived away. We had stopped charging for funerals and weddings, and instead received whatever donations people wanted to give. On balance we were no worse off, and certainly received a lot more goodwill! When they heard we didn't charge for funerals, the family said they would like to give a donation, and asked if we did anything to help the local poor. I responded by saying we were actively helping a single mother who was struggling with debt. They then made a suggestion. If they made a donation, would we be happy to open a special fund specifically to help needy people in the local area? I responded positively, and they wrote out a cheque and put it in a sealed envelope. When I got home I sat down with Penny for a cup of tea. We opened the envelope and discovered a cheque for £5,000 – as a donation for a funeral!

That incident had a big impact on the church. We had stepped forward in faith to help people in Romania, and the Lord had responded by giving back exactly the same amount. Interestingly the Lord didn't put that money back into our coffers. It was given in such a way that we had to give it away to those in need. And give it away we did. Over the next few years we made a practice of using this special fund to help families in need at Christmas. Contrary to popular opinion, charity doesn't always begin at home.

It seems to me that this is what generous love is all about. The Lord is looking for a people who will learn to give to others and trust God for their own needs. As we give away to those in need, so he gives us even more to give away. This what the apostle Paul was talking about when he said, "*You will be made rich in every way so that you can be generous on every occasion, and through us your generosity will result in thanksgiving to God.*" (2 Cor 9:11).

As I said, that donation of £5,000 had a big impact on the church. The following year we gave £10,000 to the Romania project, directly from church funds, and over the next few years church members raised a total of £60,000 to complete the project. There were many in the church who supported the project using their various gifts and abilities. Two of our members were trained chefs, while others enjoy amateur dramatics. Between us we put on some very successful Murder Mystery dinners and similar events which helped to raise the required sum. Giving is not all about money. As the church focussed on those in need, many people gave of their time, effort and expertise, including groups of people who went out to Romania to help build the school and share their faith in Christ.

CONCLUSION

What can we learn from this church that learned to give? I would suggest that the experience of Broad Haven shows that the biblical principles of giving actually work in practice. The deepest impact came from the fact that these were not stories happening to another church in another country in another time - they were happening to us here and now. Suddenly God was becoming very real, and for some people this was their first experience of God stepping into their lives in a significant way.

There was also the 'church' factor. It's one thing to hear of occasional stories like this happening to a friend or acquaintance, but when the church started hearing regular testimonies of

God providing in a miraculous way, at Sunday services, church meetings, Bible study groups and in the church newsletter, the impact was magnified.

Of course there were many blessings that had nothing to do with finance. As people began to sense they were on an adventure with God, there was a greater excitement and expectancy, with an increased openness and more positive response to new initiatives. The numbers of people coming to midweek Bible study grew from the half a dozen that used to meet in the vestry, to 60 or 70 meeting in various housegroups. The level of prayer went up, not just in housegroups, but as we started having a time of open prayer in Sunday services and church meetings. It was so heartening to hear young Christians praying out loud with uncomplicated language straight from the heart, alongside older Christians who had never prayed out loud before, who were now opening their hearts in prayer before the whole church.

When the church made its initial decision to double its offering and call a minister, it was a huge step of faith. So too was the decision to tithe the church offering, and later to increase the giving by a third in order to call a second minister. The faith that was so evident in those decisions grew year by year as God provided in amazing ways and the whole church learned to 'revere the Lord their God.' Once people grew in their faith that God could and would provide, their faith grew in other areas. In the possibility of healing prayer; the possibility that God might use someone's words to help a friend come to faith; the possibility that God might speak clearly to guide someone; that God might open the door if someone stepped out in faith as they felt led.

A clear expression of the growth in personal faith was the growing numbers of people who were being saved and baptised. On most occasions those being baptised would give a personal testimony and it became quite common for someone in their testimony to say they had been to a previous baptism, and God had spoken to them through someone else's testimony. Sometimes it felt as if we were on a roll, as when we baptised 22 adults in 22 months, which was huge for a little village chapel like ours. And of course, a greater level of faith led to even more blessing which again lifted our faith.

I do recognise that of course there were other factors involved, and none of this happened overnight. As I say, it was four years after I first preached on tithing before the church meeting agreed to tithe the church income. And the stories I've shared here happened over a period of 21 years. But I have no doubt in my mind that God honoured this church that was willing to step out in faith when they doubled the offering, and then continued to walk by faith as they learned to give.

Some years ago I visited a large church which was known for its 'culture of honour', a value that had been taught, practised and then instilled in the DNA of the church. What happened at Broad Haven, with God's help, was that over time we established a culture of generous love, which became very much a part of the DNA of the church.

15 The Joy of Giving

It was Christmas morning, and we were on our way home after taking the service at a local village chapel in Breconshire. My daughter Lucy and her husband Timo were with me, and the rest of the family were a little way behind in another car. Having just preached a joyful Christmas message, and now heading home for a family Christmas with all the trimmings, I was full of the Christmas spirit and 'goodwill towards man'. As we came into the village we saw a young couple thumbing a lift in the opposite direction. There weren't many cars about that Christmas morning, and a hundred yards down the road I pulled into a layby and turned the car around.

"What are you doing, Dad?" asked Lucy.

"We're going to give a lift to that young couple."

"But they're going in the opposite direction. Mum's cooking Christmas dinner!"

"It's Christmas!" I said, "We can't leave them standing there in the cold and wet. Anyway, it won't take long,"

I was too full of Christmas spirit to worry about how long it might take. Having just preached on the Christmas message of 'goodwill towards man', I now had an opportunity to put that message into practice, and I felt quite elated. I pulled up and they jumped in.

Our passengers turned out to be a young French couple who had signed on to work for a few months in a posh hotel five miles down the road. They were due there shortly to work in the kitchen, preparing Christmas dinner for all the guests. Lucy and Timo both speak French, and the car was soon filled with laughter and chatter, as though we'd known them for years. They were so grateful to be saved a five mile walk in the cold and wet, and as we drove away from the hotel, I felt a lovely warm feeling inside. Lots of good things awaited us at home. Family and grandchildren, food, presents, laughter, sitting around the fire listening to the Queen's Speech, and plenty of time to relax and take it all in. But the joy in my heart came from knowing that we'd been able to help someone. That we'd given of our time and effort to do someone a good turn. That even though we'd probably never see them again, there was a young couple who were so grateful for the one car, going in the opposite direction, which turned around and gave them a lift on Christmas morning.

Okay, perhaps I'm being a little self-indulgent. It was no great sacrifice, we were only twenty minutes late getting home, and I enjoyed helping them.

But isn't that the point? I enjoyed it. God loves a cheerful giver! God wants us all to experience the sheer joy of blessing other people. Even – and especially – complete strangers. Whether we give our time, effort, or money, God wants us to think beyond ourselves and to experience the delight that comes from blessing others. God loves to bless. He delights in it. It's the ultimate 'feel good factor'. Most of the time we are robbed of that feel good factor, by believing the lie that it is more blessed to receive than to give. What if it's the other way round? What if the happiest person on Christmas morning is Father Christmas himself?

Have you ever wondered what it would feel like to be Father Christmas? Going from house to house on Christmas Eve, secretly leaving presents that will bring great joy and delight to so many people the next morning?

It happened to me one Christmas Eve in Broad Haven. Remember how the church gave £5,000 to a project in Romania, and a week or so later we received a £5,000 donation for a funeral? That donation came with specific instructions. We were asked to set up a special fund to be used to help needy families and individuals in the locality. After some discussion at the Deacons meeting we decided that as well as using the fund as and when the need arose, we would also draw up a list of needy families every December, and give each one some money for Christmas.

One year we had drawn up a list of about half a dozen families or individuals, and decided to give each one a Christmas card with £100 in cash. The card would be signed from the church, with some appropriate words inside. So far so good. The problem was that Christmas can be a really busy time for a church pastor, especially when you have five children, all with their separate school Christmas events, not to mention the numerous carol services, Christmas dinners and special services. It was my job to write out and deliver these special Christmas cards around the village, but it got put off and put off because I had so many other things to do. I seem to remember that Christmas Eve, I was still buying last minute presents for the family, and then I had to prepare for our two Christmas Eve events.

First was the 7pm Carol Service in the Galleon, the local pub. Over the years this had become a local tradition, and for many families in the village this was when Christmas really began. I say families because many years before, the landlord had the idea of having Father Christmas come to the pub and hand out presents to the kids on Christmas Eve. To make it more Christmassy they asked me to come and lead some carols. I was unsure at first because I didn't particularly want to encourage children into the pub, but I decided that if the parents were taking their children anyway, then why not? The first year it was a few carols; the second year it was well known carols with some readings telling the story, and in no time at all it was the Christmas story with readings and carols, a crowded pub with everyone having a carol sheet in one hand and a drink in the other, me with a microphone in my hand, sharing an appropriate testimony, and praying for everyone present. Then Father Christmas would come in out of the cold and sit by the roaring fire, handing out presents to the children, while I sat at the bar having a drink and some really interesting conversations. The landlord claimed it was his busiest night of the year; it was certainly packed. Later that evening we would be in the chapel for Christmas Eve Communion, finishing just after midnight and wishing each other a Happy Christmas as we trooped home in the frosty dark.

I can't remember when exactly I managed to deliver the cards. It was either after the pub before the communion service, or it may even have been after the communion, in the early hours of Christmas morning. It was certainly dark, and far too late to go knocking on doors, so I simply went round the village, slipping these cards through the letter box. I knew all the people involved, and as I walked round I imagined the scene next morning, as these lovely people picked up an envelope, wondering who had dropped a card through the door on Christmas morning, and opened the card to find a gift which I know would have brought tears to their eyes. It was then that I knew what it must feel like to be Father Christmas. To experience the joy of giving so much pleasure to so many people at the same time, must rank as one of the greatest 'feel good' factors of all time.

I happen to think that the legend of jolly Father Christmas with his reindeer and sleigh has robbed the church of something special. It's taken away the message that actually it's Father God who is full of joy. It's Father God who loves to give. It's Father God who loves to bring families together and to turn the hearts of the parents to the children, and the hearts of the children to the parents; it's Father God who initiates all the love, peace and goodwill that we associate with Christmas. A peace and goodwill that touched the trenches of the Western Front on Christmas Day 1914, and caused war weary soldiers to lay down their weapons and play football with the enemy just for one day, because it was Christmas.

The core message of Christmas, when we give to others to celebrate God's gift of his Son, is not just for one day, once a year; it's for every day, all year round. And I'm determined to shout that message from the rooftops. The joy of giving and blessing other people is not just for Christmas, it's for life! And if we learn to practice this God-given lifestyle on a regular basis, we can be transformed.

Consider the case of Ebenezer Scrooge from Charles Dickens' 'A Christmas Carol'. Here was a man who hated Christmas for one simple reason. He hated to give. He was the original Mr 'Take and Keep' and he couldn't give or share to save his life. For him there was only one word to describe Christmas – humbug! The thought of giving his office clerk Bob Cratchit a day off for Christmas was agony to his soul, and he certainly wasn't letting him go home early just because it was Christmas Eve. The weather outside could be freezing but the maximum allowance on the office fire was only one lump of coal at a time. And when everyone else went to bed on Christmas Eve filled with excitement and anticipation, old Ebenezer Scrooge felt more miserable and grumpy than ever.

Then it happened. A visitation on Christmas night. A challenge to his mind and heart. A visit to the poor in the shape of Bob Cratchit's poor family and disabled son, Tiny Tim. An opportunity to feel compassion… and Ebenezer Scrooge experienced a heart transplant. There is no other way to describe it. He wakes up in the morning with an absolute and complete change of heart. He goes out into the street shouting Happy Christmas to all and sundry. He goes to the butchers and buys the biggest turkey in the shop. He takes it to Bob Cratchit to share with his family, and for the first time in his life, Ebenezer Scrooge is filled with joy. He is filled with joy because he has learned to give.

Please forgive the overdose on Christmas. If you're reading this on a beach in the summer holidays it may seem out of place. But delivering gifts on Christmas Eve at the dead of night is when it really came home to me. It is so much fun to give.

The joy of giving to others is only matched by seeing others learning to do the same. Back at Broad Haven, God poured out his blessing one Sunday morning.

My daughter Katie had taken a year out after A-levels to work on an Oasis project with a small church in Uganda. This church, pastored by John Okello, had a wonderful heart for the poor, and John and his church members had built a school for orphans with their bare hands. These children had been destined for a life of hunger and destitution, but with education they could hopefully grow up to find employment and a better life. After the initial contact through Katie's gap year, the church at Broad Haven decided to support the Ugandan church and school on a long term basis. John employed professional teachers, but there was no support from the state, so John had to raise the funding himself. Part of this was done through the children making beautiful necklaces and bracelets from beads made out of paper. John would send over big packs of this jewellery, and we would sell it locally and send the money back to John, as well as supporting the work through our own church funds.

One day John sent an email asking for urgent prayer. The school was built on rented land, and the opportunist landlord had decided to take the land back, together with the school building. John and the church were powerless and could do nothing to stop him. They were determined to build another school as soon as possible, but they didn't want to make the same mistake twice, so this time they were going to buy the land first. They had found an ideal plot of land nearby, but it cost £3,000, which was an astronomical figure for their small church. John asked us to pray that somehow they would find the money to buy the land and build a new school, as quickly as possible.

We printed John's email in our weekly newsletter, which the congregation received as they came into church on Sunday morning. No mention of it was made during the service, but obviously one or two had read the details, as it was mentioned in our time of open prayer. Tony was sitting up in the balcony, and he had a very down to earth way of praying. Short and sweet, and very much to the point. "God,' he said, 'John Okello needs £3,000 to buy a plot of land and build a new school. I pray that this church will give the money."

I was in the pulpit at the time, and I was rather taken aback by Tony's prayer, but we carried on with the service, and nothing more was said. We had coffee in the Village Hall afterwards, and a young couple came up to speak to me. They had been very moved by Tony's prayer, and wanted to give some money in response. "No problem." I said, "You decide how much you want to give, and I'm sure the church will respond as well, and we can send it over in one lump sum."

"No," they said. "You don't understand. We want to give the full £3,000. When Tony prayed, God spoke to us individually at the same time, and we just looked at each other and said, 'Yes." I thanked them both for their generosity, and turned round to find someone else also wanting to give money for the plot of land. I can't remember how many people approached me that morning, but by the end of the week our treasurer was able to send John £5,000 to buy the land and purchase materials to build the school. Years later we are still in touch with John, and the school is going from strength to strength.

There was no discussion or decision at a church meeting. People saw the need, they wanted to give, and they responded generously, from the heart. It felt good. Very good.

Over the years as we began to practice giving in a deeper way, the realisation grew that it's good to give. Not just good for those who receive, but quite wonderful for those who give. Do you know why God loves a cheerful giver? Because a cheerful giver is someone who gets it. Someone who has discovered the very heart of the Gospel. That God so loved the world he gave his Son; that Jesus so loved the world he gave his life; that Jesus calls us to love, and give, and bless one another as he has loved us. Generous love. And as we give in such a way that others are blessed, we experience the life that we were created to live. Like an engine that has been repaired and properly serviced, and is now running beautifully. This is how we were meant to live.

Go therefore, and do likewise.

APPENDIX:
BIBLE VERSES ON GIVING
AND RELATED THEMES

This is not an exhaustive list, simply some key verses that struck me on my biblical journey, together with my own comments. (For a comprehensive list of the Bible's 700 verses on money, and the 2,350 verses on money, wealth and possessions, see Mark Lloydbottom's *'Foundation Truth'*, a free download at www.yourmoneycounts.org.uk)

Gen 1:29	God gives generously, providing all that we need for life
Gen 3:6	Man's fallen nature – he takes what does not belong to him
Gen 4:3-5	Cain gives without thought, but Abel gives the biggest and best
Gen 14:20	The first mention of tithing, as a spontaneous act of gratitude to God
Gen 22:1-18	Abraham's worship, sacrifice, obedience and faith, leads to blessing
Gen 28:20-22	In response to God's protection and provision, Jacob promises to tithe
Ex 25:1,2	The Israelites are commanded to give as their hearts prompt them
Ex 35,36	God's people giving willingly and generously for the Tabernacle

Lev 27:30	The tithe belongs to God, just as income tax belongs to the Revenue
Dt 14:22-29	The command to tithe, and the benefits of tithing
Dt 15:7-11	Do not be hardhearted and tightfisted, but give with open hands
1 Sam 8:10-17	Israel's kings will take and take - because they have the power
2 Sam 24:24	David refuses to offer a sacrifice that costs him nothing
Neh 13:10-12	Tithes are withheld, and God's house is neglected
Prov 3:9,10	Honour the Lord with your wealth and you will be blessed
Prov 11:24,25	A generous man will prosper
Prov 28:27	Give to the poor and be blessed. Ignore the poor and be cursed
Mal 3:7-12	Do not rob God. Bring the whole tithe and you will be blessed
Matt 6:2-4	Give in secret and humility, and your Father will reward you
Matt 6:19-33	You cannot serve both God and money. Put God first in your heart
Matt 7:11	'How much more' will the Father give to those who ask
Matt 7:12	The Golden Rule – do to others what you would have them do to you
Matt 10:7-10	Freely receive, and freely give. Trust God to provide.

Matt 19:16-24	The rich young man. It is hard for the rich to enter the Kingdom
Matt 23:23	Practice justice, mercy, and faithfulness, and do not neglect to tithe
Matt 25:31-46	The Sheep and the Goats – what we do for others, we do for Jesus
Mk 12:41-44	Jesus honours the widow who gave all she had to God
Lk 6:30	Give to those who ask you.
Lk 6:38	As we give to others, so it will be given to us
Lk 10:4-8	Receive what is given you
Lk 10:25-37	The Good Samaritan – love your neighbour as you love yourself
Lk 12:13-21	Put your security in God, not in your wealth and possessions
Lk 12:31-34	Seek first his Kingdom, sell your possessions and give to the poor
Lk 16:19-31	Parable of the rich man and Lazarus.
Jn 3:16	God loved the world so much, he gave…
Jn 6:1-13	A boy gives what he has; God adds the blessing; the hungry are fed
Acts 2:44,45	Selling possessions and goods they gave to anyone in need
Acts 4:32-5v5	Generous giving comes from the heart, not from a desire to impress
Acts 11:27-30	Response to the famine in Judea - an early example of Christian Aid
Ro 12:8	The spiritual gift of generosity

1 Cor 16:1,2	Every Sunday, give a proportion of your income
2 Cor 8:1-7	The grace and generosity of the impoverished church in Macedonia
2 Cor 9:6-15	Sow generously and you will reap generously
Php 4:15-19	God meets our needs as we meet the needs of others
1 Tim 6:10	The love of money is a root of all kinds of evil
1 Tim 6:17-19	The rich are commanded to trust God and to be generous to the poor
Jas 2:1-17	Put your faith into action and care for the poor
Jas 5:1-6	Those living in luxury are condemned for cheating the poor
1 Jn 3:17	Real love for God includes compassion for the poor
Rev 22:17	The free gift of the water of life

 **GENEROUS HEART**

I do hope you've enjoyed **OPEN HANDS OPEN HEART**. You may want to develop some of the issues a little further either in your small groups, church group or in your personal life. If so, **GENEROUS HEART** may be able to help.

We provide a wide range of materials to help you which include seminars allowing you to explore these principles further.

A visit to our web site will provide details of all our resources and other books, videos and programmes.

It would be good to hear from you.

Philip Bishop

For further information visit
www.generousheart.co.uk

or email Philip Bishop at
philbish1959@gmail.com

To contact Ifor Williams direct, email:
iforwilliams937@gmail.com

Lightning Source UK Ltd.
Milton Keynes UK
UKOW05f2004050717
304763UK00001B/55/P